GORKY

GORKY

HENRI TROYAT
Translated by Lowell Bair

CROWN PUBLISHERS, INC. · NEW YORK

Published by Crown Publishers, Inc., 225 Park Avenue South, New York, New York 10003.

First published in France as *Gorki* by Librarie Ernest Flammarion

Copyright © 1986 by Flammarion

CROWN is a trademark of Crown Publishers, Inc.

Printed in the U.S.A.

Library of Congress Cataloging-in-Publication Data

Troyat, Henri, 1911–
  [Gorki. English]
  Gorky / Henri Troyat; translated by Lowell Bair.
    p. cm.
  Translation of: Gorki.
  Bibliography: p.
  Includes index.
  1. Gorky, Maksim, 1868–1936—Biography. 2. Authors, Russian—20th century—Biography. I. Title.
PG3465.T7613 1989
891.78'309—dc19
[B]   88–37627
                                        CIP

ISBN 0-517-57237-0

Design by Lauren Dong

10 9 8 7 6 5 4 3 2 1

First Edition

CONTENTS

GORKY

1

HUMBLE ORIGINS

Stubborn and conceited, Vasily Kashirin had decided once and for all that his daughter Varvara would marry a man of high rank, a "hereditary gentleman." In his youth he had pulled barges on the Volga, and later, by dint of hard work and thrift, he had succeeded in establishing a profitable dye shop in Nizhni Novgorod. He now took pride in holding the honorary position of dean of the dyers' guild in that old city at the confluence of the Volga and the Oka. His ambitions for Varvara's future were justified, he felt, by his affluence and his connections in middle-class society.

She was pretty and educated, but she had an impassioned nature. When she fell in love with Maxim Savvatievich Peshkov, an ordinary carpenter who worked in a shipyard, she braved her father's indignation at the thought of such a mismatch and married that lowly suitor. Furious at being disobeyed, Vasily Kashirin refused to let her set foot in his house. For several years she went on living in Nizhni Novgorod, happy to have a sober, hard-working, loving, and cheerful husband, and unhappy at being rejected by her family.

After having three children who died in infancy, on March 16, 1868,[1] she gave birth to a vigorous baby boy. The future Maxim Gorky was christened on March 22, with the first name of Alexey. Three years later, Maxim Savvatievich Peshkov was given the post of wharf manager in Astrakhan and moved there with his little family. Soon after they settled into their new home there was an outbreak of cholera, which struck Alexey when he was four. He was lucky enough to recover from it, with the help of diligent care, but his father caught it from him and died almost immediately, at the age of thirty-one. During this time Varvara gave birth to another son, Maxim.

Widowed and destitute, she had no choice but to go back to her parents in Nizhni Novgorod. With Alexey and Maxim she boarded a steamboat for the trip up the Volga. But little Maxim died on the way and was buried at Saratov. Meanwhile, Vasily Kashirin had forgiven his daughter. In spite of his brutal and miserly character, he took her and her one surviving child into his house with good grace.

What should have been a refuge for her quickly became a hell. Her father was now embittered because his small-scale business was declining as a result of technological progress. New dye shops, using improved machines, were drawing away more and more of his customers. Feeling that he was headed for ruin, he held the whole world responsible for it. Besides Varvara and Alexey, his sons Yakov and Mikhail, with their wives and children, were also living in his house.

Always drunk and abusive, the two brothers quarreled with each other and badgered their father, trying to make him divide the family property between them. They wanted to go into business on their own and were afraid Varvara would demand her dowry. It rightfully belonged to her, but her father had withheld it to punish her for marrying against his will. "The hatred that each had for the others filled my grandfather's house like a thick fog," Gorky was to write. "It poisoned the adults, and even the children shared it."[2] Quarrels usually broke out when the family gathered for a meal. Once, during dinner, when a discussion had suddenly turned acrimonious, the two brothers leapt to their feet, rushed at each other shouting insults and began wrestling on the floor. Their father pounded the table with his spoon and loudly ordered them to stop, the women shrieked, the children cried, and the shop foremen came running in to separate the combatants and tie their hands with towels.

Little Alexey was fascinated by his grandfather, a gaunt old man with a hawklike profile, a red goatee, and piercing green eyes. Besides being curious about him, he was also afraid of him. Vasily Kashirin was a believer, and practiced religion in his fashion. The God he served with punctilious devotion was a God of rigor, rancor, and vengeance. Inspired by that fulminating Jehovah, he did not hesitate to punish his grandchildren for the slightest misstep by beating them till he drew blood.

Once, possessed by fury, he whipped Alexey with long willow rods, holding him across his knees. The boy struggled and screamed while Varvara wrung her hands and moaned, "Papa, you mustn't! Give him to me!" With his face convulsed, the old man roared, "I'll kill him!" and went on lacerating Alexey's back. He did not stop until his victim lost consciousness. Alexey was carried to a little bedroom full of icons and spent several days lying on his stomach in a soft bed. That punishment left its mark on him for the rest of his life. "As if it had been flayed," he wrote, "my heart became extraordinarily sensitive to the slightest offense or suffering, whether it was inflicted on me or someone else."

Vasily Kashirin's fits of insane rage were interspersed with periods of affectionate calm. During those periods he liked to tell about the days when he had pulled barges on the Volga, staggering with fatigue. Alexey was captivated as he listened. "I nearly wept at having to remember that it was he who had so cruelly beaten me, but I could not forget it." And when his irascible, envious, and greedy Uncle Yakov sang a folk song, accompanying himself on the guitar, the boy wondered how such sweet music could come from that drunken brute. He was already realizing confusedly that people were a mixture of base instincts and noble impulses, and that no one was completely innocent or completely guilty.

This impression was strengthened in him by the long conversations he had with his grandmother. Ponderously fat and stooped almost to the point of being hunchbacked, she had a good-natured face with a big, red, porous nose and bright, cheerful eyes. She too was a firm believer, but her God, unlike her husband's, was a God of gentleness, pity, and forgiveness. In a low, mysterious voice, she told her grandson stories of good-hearted bandits, miracle-working saints, and evil spirits infesting forests, ponds, and stables. "It seemed to me that before I knew her I had been asleep, plunged in darkness. . . . Her selfless love of the world enriched me and filled me with vigor for a difficult life." Day after day, speaking straight from her simple heart, she taught him compassion for the downtrodden, wonder at the everyday world, and the pleasure of using the colloquial language of the Russian people. Without knowing it, she wanted him to be, like her, a storyteller in command of words with magic power.

She was much closer to him than his mother, who, still young and attractive, found her early widowhood hard to bear and often slipped out of the house to carry on amorous affairs. She soon remarried. Her new husband was an idler with elegant manners, ten years younger than herself. Their first child died in infancy shortly after the birth of their second, who also failed to survive.

Meanwhile, Alexey had been placed in a primary school. He arrived the first day wearing a pair of his mother's shoes, a yellow shirt, and a coat assembled from one of his grandmother's smocks. The other children made fun of him. He stoically put up with it, but could not endure the reprimands of the schoolmaster and the Orthodox priest who had the task of teaching the catechism to those high-spirited little demons. The schoolmaster often sent him home for misconduct, and there his grandfather methodically thrashed him. Sometimes it was his mother who beat him, to calm her nerves.

One evening she and her husband quarreled in his presence. Her husband knocked her to her knees and began kicking her in the chest. She groaned with her head turned away from him. Excited by her distress, his eyes shining, he kicked her still harder. Horrified, Alexey took a knife from the table and stabbed at his stepfather's side with all his might. Luckily the blade only slashed his clothes and scratched his skin. He ran from the room, howling. At first Varvara berated her son, but later she hugged and kissed him and murmured, "Forgive me, it was my fault. My darling boy, how could you.... With a knife!" He told her he would have killed his stepfather without mercy, and then himself. "When I recall such horrible episodes, which reflect so well the savagery of Russian ways, heavy as lead," wrote Gorky, "I sometimes ask myself if it is good to speak of them. And, with renewed self-assurance, I answer myself: 'Yes.' For that ignoble, long-lived truth is still a truth today. We must know it thoroughly, down to its roots, so that we can tear out those roots from our memories, from our souls, from our appalling, squalid lives."

Since his grandfather's business was still deteriorating and the family was short of money, his grandmother spent a good part of her time doing embroidery. After school, and on Sundays and holidays, he gathered bones, rags, nails, and paper from streets and backyards. Every Saturday he sold his harvest to junkmen for a few kopecks and gave the money to his grandmother. She would put the coins in her pocket and thank him with tears in her eyes. At school his classmates jeered at him, calling him "ragpicker" and "beggar," and told the schoolmaster they could not sit next to him because he smelled like a garbage dump. Humiliated in public, he suffered all the more from that accusation of dirtiness because he carefully washed himself every morning and never went to school in the clothes he wore when he gathered junk.

He soon went on to activities that were more lucrative but less lawful. Having formed a gang of boys as poor as he was, he began stealing posts and boards from lumberyards on the banks of the river. "In our part of town, stealing was not considered a crime. It was a habit, and almost the only means of subsistence for people who did not always have enough to eat. . . . On Sundays the men bragged of their exploits; the children listened to them and took advantage of the lesson." To steal from the lumberyards, the boys had to elude the vigilance of the watchmen and drag the posts and boards across ice and snow. With the money they got from selling them, they bought bread, sugar, and tea.

These thefts did not prevent Alexey from continuing his studies. He was attracted to books. One day he stole a ruble from his mother to buy a book of Bible stories and a volume of Andersen's tales. She discovered it, beat him "with a kitchen utensil," then forgave him, weeping. From her school days, she had kept a respect for the printed word. She taught her son the poems she had loved, but when he recited them he altered them by adding words of his own, taken from the language of the people. In the evening, lying in the garret with his grandmother, he recited comical verses of his composition that made her burst out laughing.

He had such a keen mind that his grades at school were judged satisfactory in spite of his mischievous behavior. In 1878, when he was ten, he did so well in his third-grade final examinations that he was given an honor certificate and a prize consisting of three books: the Gospels, Krylov's *Fables*, and a paperbacked book with an incomprehensible title: *Fata Morgana*. He took them to a bookshop, sold them, and gave the money—fifty-five kopecks—to his grandmother. As for the honor certificate, he dirtied it and covered it with disrespectful inscriptions to show his contempt for school.

This was his farewell to formal education. Relieved at not having to go back to the classroom, he had no idea that he would later regret his lack of schooling and suffer from an inferiority complex with regard to people who had gone to a university. His almost religious respect for "knowledge" was to be complicated all through his life by an instinctive animosity against intellectuals who had not come from the people.

At home, however, idleness, poverty, and quarreling created such a climate of despair that he soon began to miss school. His stepfather had disappeared, abandoning Varvara after squandering her meager dowry. On the verge of ruin, the family now lived in a dark, cramped basement.

Varvara was gravely ill. In the last stage of tuberculosis, she had become "long and thin as a fir tree with its branches broken off." Her breathing was wheezy, her lips were blue. On August 5, 1879, when Alexey came back from an errand, he found her sitting at the table, wearing a violet dress, with a look of angry dignity on her face.

"Come here!" she said to him harshly. "Where have you been?"

Without waiting for an answer, she grabbed him by the hair with her left hand and, with her right, picked up a long, flexible knife made from a saw blade and hit him with the flat of it. Then she lay down on her bed, wiped the sweat from her forehead with a handkerchief, and asked for water. Alexey gave her some in a cup. She took a sip of it, turned her eyes toward the icons, opened her mouth and, with a surprised expression, breathed her last. For a long time Alexey stood beside the bed with the cup in his hand, staring at the dead woman's face as it sagged and turned gray.

A few days after his mother's funeral, his grandfather said to him, "Alexey, you're not a medal: you can't go on hanging from my neck. Go out into the world and earn your own living."

Alexey was eleven. He obeyed.

2

THE VOLGA

Left to his own devices, Alexey first went to work as an errand boy in a shoe store owned by a man named Porkhunov. He quickly became indignant at the venomous servility of Porkhunov and his salesclerks, who greeted their women customers with obsequious bows, then talked about them in crude, abusive terms as soon as they left. For a few kopecks he polished the shoes of everyone who worked in the store, started the samovar, swept the floor, brought in firewood, and delivered packages all over town. Exasperated and overworked, he was already thinking of leaving when one day he knocked over a pot of soup, scalded his hand, and had to be taken to a hospital.

This accident marked the end of his apprenticeship in the shoe store. After a few days of treatment in the hospital, he went back to his grandparents' house and was greeted sarcastically by his grandfather: "Hello, Your Reverence, Your

Highness! You've already finished your time of service? Well, then, now you can live as you please!"[1]

His grandmother told him that his grandfather was completely ruined and that God had punished him for his stinginess. "We lost our money because we didn't help the poor or pity the unfortunate," she said. In the hope of expiating that sin and regaining God's favor, she sometimes got up in the middle of the night and gave "secret alms." Holding Alexey by the hand, she slipped through the dark, deserted streets, stopped at the poorest houses, and after crossing herself three times, left packets of three hard biscuits on the windowsills. They also went into the forest together, in summer and fall, to gather berries, mushrooms, and herbs, which they sold to merchants, keeping part of the money for their "secret alms."

These forest outings delighted Alexey. In the shade of the trees he savored deep inner peace and felt himself developing the ability to single out each rustling of nature. "My sight and hearing were sharpened," he later wrote, "my memory improved, my feelings deepened." Because of her wisdom and kindness, and her harmony with heavenly powers, he regarded his grandmother as a superior being. At the same time, he felt it would be "good to be a bandit, to rob rich misers and give their money to the poor." He was inclined toward both revolt and compassion. Sometimes he was eager to fight against injustice, coarseness, poverty, and stupidity, and sometimes he wanted to console their victims. He was outraged by some of the things he overheard: "We can't all beat the same man at once, we have to do it one at a time," or "Didn't God create women so men could have fun with them?"

From the age of twelve, he felt for women a kind of amazed pity and reverent wonder. He became friends with a little lame girl, "lively as a warbler," who loved reading and drove the boys wild with the "blue flame" of her eyes. They all bragged in front of her about their prowess in the game of ninepins, and sometimes they even fought to win her admiration. Alexey was secretly jealous.

His grandfather soon decreed that he had lolled around long enough and that it was time he went back "into the world." He was apprenticed to a draftsman named Sergeyev, who worked for a construction firm. Instead of teaching him the trade, Sergeyev put him in his wife's service. A loud, ill-tempered woman, she made Alexey wash the floors, scour pots and pans, split kindling, and peel vegetables, and she took him to the market with her to carry her food baskets. She detested her mother-in-law, and all day long the two women exchanged insults, threats, and hysterical outbursts. During one of those clashes, Sergeyev's wife picked up a kitchen knife, locked herself in the bathroom, and began shrieking savagely. Sergeyev leaned against the door and lifted Alexey to his shoulders so that he could reach the transom. "Break the glass," he ordered, "and unlock the door." Alexey broke the glass and leaned inside, but Sergeyev's wife hit him on the head with the handle of the knife. She was ousted from her lair only with great difficulty.

She and her mother-in-law were in agreement only when it came to berating Alexey. When Sergeyev gave in to his clerk's requests and began trying to teach Alexey draftsmanship, his mother poured kvass on all the drawings. Another time, with a malicious grimace, she spilled lamp oil on them. Hard-hearted though they were, the two shrews were steeped in piety. During their quarrels, each of them invoked the Lord and prayed for Him to inflict horrendous calamities on the other. Their God was crafty, vindictive, and narrow-minded, like the God of Alexey's grandfather.

Alexey went to church with them for Saturday evening services and Sunday mass. There, amid the bluish smoke of incense, the flickering candles, and the Byzantine gildings of the icons, all the women looked like angels. Lulled by the solemn singing of the choir, he became detached from sordid everyday reality. "It was good to be in church. I rested there, as I did in the forest and the fields. My childish heart, which had already known so many humiliations and been soiled by the ferocious brutality of life, was suffused with ardent, chaotic dreams." Meditating on his fate, he sometimes composed his own prayers. Words would gather themselves into a kind of plaintive poem: "Lord, Lord, I'm so bored! Please let me grow up quickly. I can't face living any more. Sergeyev's wife is a puppet of the devil. She howls like a wolf in the woods. Living is a very bitter thing!"

But often, instead of going to Saturday evening services, he slipped away and strolled along the streets, looking in through lighted windows at the lives of all those strangers unaware of his presence. "The windows showed me many different pictures. I saw people praying, kissing, fighting, playing cards, having silent discussions with worried looks on their faces. As in a one-kopeck panorama, a mute, fishlike life unfolded in front of me." Without knowing it, he was already constructing novels in his head.

He thought more and more seriously about leaving, but the winter cold kept him with his employers, living "like a rat in a cellar." It was not until spring that he carried out his plan. When he was sent to buy bread, with twenty kopecks in his pocket, he ran away. But instead of going back to his grandfather, whose violence he feared, he began living on the bank of the Volga, sleeping on the bare ground with the stevedores and eating their leftovers. After three days, one of them told him that a mess boy was wanted on the steamboat *Dobry* ("Good").

He boarded the *Dobry* at the age of twelve. For a salary of two rubles a month, he worked from six in the morning till midnight, in the steam and noise of the galley. But sometimes he went up on deck and, with a pang in his heart, admired the vast, peaceful landscape of the Volga. The majesty of the river marked him for life. "At night," he wrote, "the moon made a streak of light from the ship to the meadows on shore. The old reddish steamer, with a white band around her smokestack, moved along unhurriedly. Her paddlewheel flailed at the silvery water with uneven movements. The dark banks came toward her, casting their shadows on the water, dotted with red lights from the windows of peasant houses. There was singing in a village, and the refrain, 'Ai liuli,' sounded like 'Hallelujah'. . . . The beauty of the night moved me to tears." The *Dobry* towed a heavy barge at the end of a long cable. Around the deck of the barge was a metal fence that enclosed a group of moving shadows: convicts headed for exile or prison. At the bow was a sentry whose bayonet gleamed in the moonlight. Confined in their cage, the convicts almost admired the tranquil night.

The cook Alexey worked for, a good-natured man named Smoury, took a liking to him. He loved books and had a collection of them in his black ironbound trunk. But he had a rudimentary mind and did not know how to be selective in his reading. Jumbled together in his little library were *The Precepts of Omir, Memoirs of an Artilleryman, Letters of Lord Sedengall*, and a *Treatise on the Bedbug, a Harmful Insect, and Its Extermination*. He had Alexey take time off from work to read these books aloud to him. The captain's wife, who was more cultivated, soon lent Smoury other books. Among them was Gogol's short novel *Taras Bulba*. Alexey read it to Smoury and they both wept with emotion.

The more the cook became attached to Alexey, however, the more the rest of the crew were hostile to the boy. They hated and insulted Smoury's "pet" because he liked books, was discreet, did not drink, and did not tease girls during stopovers. Finally he was falsely accused of theft and ignominiously dismissed. When it was time for them to part, Smoury embraced him, gave him a multicolored beaded tobacco pouch, and said to him, "Read books, it's the best thing you can do!"

3

YEARS OF APPRENTICESHIP

When Alexey came back with eight rubles in his pocket, his grandfather greeted him with insults. Exasperated, the boy butted him in the stomach, making him fall backward and sit down on the floor. For a moment the old man was dazed, then he said fearfully, "You knock down your own grandfather, your mother's father?" Alexey's grandmother intervened; she pulled his hair, but halfheartedly, only for the sake of form, and told him gently, "Your grandfather is an old man. You have to respect him. And his bones are brittle!" After these words, Alexey and his grandfather were reconciled.

Alexey began earning money by catching songbirds. He spent hours in the forest, listening to their twittering and setting traps. "I was sorry to catch those little birds, and I was ashamed of shutting them up in cages. But my passion for hunting and my desire to make money overcame my compassion."[1] In the evening he gave his grandmother the birds he had caught, and the next day she went to sell them at the market.

Though the spectacle of the forest enchanted him, he was horrified by the spectacle of the street. At every step he was shocked by the bestiality of adults. Respectful of weakness, he could not bear the coarse way most men behaved with women they wanted to seduce. And when he was twelve he witnessed a rape at the foot of a wooden fence, without being seen. After the brutal copulation the woman raised herself on all fours, panting. She was naked to the waist, and when Alexey saw her big breasts hanging down it seemed to him that she had three faces. He was so deeply affected by the rape that he told a night watchman about it. Instead of being indignant, the watchman laughed. Alexey thought with horror that the same thing might have happened to his mother or grandmother.

In autumn, his grandfather decided that Alexey had done enough loafing in the streets and woods, and took him back to Sergeyev, the draftsman. And Alexey again sank into the boredom and humiliation of acting as a maid of all work. Besides doing the housework, he had to take care of the babies, wash their diapers every day, and do the other washing once a week in a public washhouse, where the women laughed at him. "Now they've turned you into a laundress!" He hit them with wet linen and they hit him back. They talked about sex as shamelessly as men. "A woman's cleverness isn't in her head," they said.

In the evening, Alexey's only diversion was to read old illustrated newspapers in the attic, where he slept on a wretched bed. But his employer's mother reproached him for wasting candles. He was reduced to collecting tallow in a sardine can and making a wick from a piece of thread.

One day, distracted by his reading, he forgot to keep an eye on the samovar. It overheated and exploded. The old woman beat him so ferociously with a bundle of pine sticks that he had to be taken to a hospital. A doctor removed forty-two

splinters from his back and spoke of having the police investigate this case of cruelty to a child. But Alexey refused to
lodge a complaint. Sergeyev thanked him and said, "I've been
beaten too, Peshkov. What beatings I used to get! And you at
least have me to sympathize with you, but I had no one, no
one at all!"

After this incident Sergeyev's mother and his wife, glad
that Alexey had not lodged a complaint, let him read as much
as he pleased.

A young neighbor, crippled and half mad, learned that
Alexey shared her love of reading and lent him some French
novels in Russian translation: Paul de Kock, Alexandre
Dumas, Ponson du Terrail, Xavier de Montépin, Emile Ga-
boriau. Carried away by the plots, he tried to imagine the
dénouements in advance. He was struck by the difference
between French life, as described in those books, and Russian life as he knew it. It seemed to him that the people were
happier, freer, and less cruel in France than in Russia. The
first book that really moved him was Edmond de Goncourt's
The Zemganno Brothers. Then he eagerly devoured Green-
wood's *True Story of a Little Waif*. Considering all that misery,
he said to himself, "So children sometimes have hard lives in
other countries. I'm not so unlucky, and I mustn't feel sorry
for myself." But it was Balzac's *Eugénie Grandet* that gave
him, at the age of thirteen, the dazzling revelation of literature. Everything in that colorful work seemed to him both true
to life and new. Old Grandet reminded him of his grandfather.
Eugénie exemplified the ideal woman: loving, suffering, and
devoted. "I realized then," Gorky wrote, "that a good and true
book is a great joy."

One evening in March 1881, when everyone in the house
was preparing to go to bed, the bells of the cathedral began
tolling mournfully. They all hurried to the windows in surprise, hoping to find out what had happened. Were the bells
sounding an alarm? Was there a fire? A war? Sergeyev went
out into the street, came back a short time later, and said

gravely, "The czar has been assassinated." Alexey wondered why someone had killed Alexander II, who had freed the serfs, and whether his son, Alexander III, who would presumably succeed him, would be equally good to the people. For two days everyone around Alexey discussed the assassination in whispers, but in answer to his questions he was told only that talking about it was prohibited. "Then it all faded away and life settled back into its humdrum routine."

Another neighbor took an interest in Alexey. She was so beautiful, elegant, and mysterious that when he looked at her he inwardly gave her the name of his favorite heroine: Queen Margot, in Dumas's novel of the same name. From her came "a sweet, strong scent of flowers, strangely mingled with a smell of horse sweat," and she looked at him dreamily from under her long lashes. She lent him Béranger's *Chansons*, translated into Russian, and Pushkin's stories and poems, which he "read all at once, with the voracity one feels before a beautiful unknown site." Queen Margot told him how Pushkin had been killed in a duel over a matter concerning his wife's honor, and she added with a bland smile, "You see how dangerous it is to love women?" He answered fervently, "It may be dangerous, but everyone falls in love."

Army officers from the local garrison often visited Queen Margot, but Alexey refused to believe that her relations with any of them went beyond flirtation: "It was hard for me to think that anyone might have a right to touch her in a daring, immodest way, to put a possessive hand on her body. I was convinced that the kind of love discussed in kitchens and the backrooms of shops was unknown to her, that she knew another kind of love, and different joys, lofty and pure." Then one day when he came to bring back a book she had lent him, he found her in bed with a man. "This is my friend," she said to him. "What are you afraid of? Come here." When he had stepped closer to her, she put her warm, sweet-smelling bare arm around his neck and murmured, "When you grow up, you'll be happy too. And now, go."

Alexey's amorous disappointment was so intense that for a moment it seemed to him that he could actually hear his heart breaking. Queen Margot went on lending him books, however, insisting that he become acquainted primarily with Russian literature. Because of her, he devoured the works of Aksakov, Odoyevsky, and Sologub, and Turgenev's *A Sportsman's Sketches*. "Those books gave me a firm, steadily growing conviction that I was not alone and would never be lost. . . . Thanks to books, I was invulnerable in many ways."

Some time later he was falsely accused of theft by a drunken soldier, and Sergeyev's mother saw to it that he was dismissed. Consumed with rage, he did not dare to go and say good-bye to Queen Margot.

After leaving Sergeyev, Alexey went to work as a mess boy on another river steamboat, the *Perm*. There he met a remarkable man named Shumov, a burly, flat-faced, curly-haired stoker and former horse thief who had traveled in Rumania, Bulgaria, Serbia, Greece, and Turkey. Shumov's philosophy of life was simple and unpolished. He knew no formal prayers, but he believed in God and addressed heaven in these terms: "Lord Jesus, have mercy on me while I'm alive, let me rest when I'm dead, and keep sickness away from me." In spite of his ugliness he was successful with women. He taught Alexey "how to handle them" but cautioned him against having sexual relations too soon. "A woman," he said, "lives on caresses the way a mushroom lives on dampness."

The stewardess tried to arouse Alexey by receiving him in her cabin, naked to the waist. But he was repelled by the sight of that flabby yellow flesh, "like old sour dough," and he hurried back to the illusions of his favorite novels. "My bookish turmoil covered me with a transparent but impenetrable cloud that protected me against the dangerous poisons of life." Alexandre Dumas's heroes inspired him with a desire to devote himself to a noble cause. His favorite character was "merry King Henry IV," "kind and close to his people."

He liked to tell Shumov about the French novels he had read. The stoker always listened attentively. One day he said, "The French have it easy."

"What do you mean?" asked Alexey.

"Take you and me, for example," replied Shumov, "we live and work in hellish heat, but they keep cool, they don't do anything except drink and stroll around. It's a pleasant life!"

"But they work too!" said Alexey.

"You'd never know it from the stories you've told me," Shumov pointed out. At these words, Alexey had a sudden realization: "All at once it became clear to me that in most of the books I had read there was never any mention of how the heroes worked or what they lived on."

With the onset of winter, the Volga froze and boat traffic was interrupted. Alexey went back to Nizhny Novgorod to look for other work and was soon apprenticed to an icon painter. The shop was filled with icons of all sizes, gilded frames, and books in Church Slavonic. A score of icon makers were crowded into a small workshop where the air was heavy with a smell of tobacco, linseed oil, varnish, and rotten eggs. Some of them were tubercular. At night they slept on the floor. Each of them had his own specialty and painted only one detail of an icon, without concerning himself with the whole. They liked to sing sad songs together. Only vodka was able to cheer them up. They would then burst into wild, disquieting exhilaration. "Too often," wrote Gorky, "Russian gaiety unexpectedly turns to cruelty and tragedy. A man dances as though breaking his chains, then suddenly he frees a ferocious beast inside himself and, seized with frenzied anguish, hurls himself at everyone he sees, tearing, biting, destroying."

Young Alexey was irritated by those irrational shifts from excessive melancholy to excessive joy. He wanted to see the icon painters simply and sanely happy now and then. To entertain them, he told them the stories he had read. Later he got a few books and read aloud, before all those heads sedately leaning over meticulous work. "I liked them at those times, and they were good to me. I felt at home with them."

As he came to know his companions in drudgery better, he was surprised that so much talent was combined with so much ignorance in those roughhewn men. "I sometimes thought they must be joking when they said that England was on the other side of the Atlantic, or that Napoleon was of Russian origin, from a noble family in Kaluga. When I told them what I had seen with my own eyes, they scarcely believed me, but they all liked wondrous or horrifying fairy tales. Even the old ones preferred fiction to truth. . . . In general, reality did not interest them and they took a dreamy view of the future, refusing to see the poverty and ugliness of the present."

Alexey would have liked to learn the trade of painting, but the owner of the shop assigned him to the salesroom as an assistant clerk. His new work displeased him because it required him to deceive customers about the value of the merchandise. Sometimes the manager of the salesroom would buy an ancient icon from an old peasant for next to nothing, or sell him a recent psalter at an outrageous price. Alexey would watch the scene in heavyhearted silence, a prisoner of his role behind the counter. He felt sorry for those surly, stingy, "ratlike" peasants when they sacrificed their last rubles for a commonplace icon. He wished he could whisper to them the real value of the article being praised by the salesroom manager.

Among the customers were many Old Believers, who detested the official Orthodox church, lived in closed communities, and worshiped in accordance with texts and rituals dating from before the reforms introduced by the Patriarch Nikon in 1654. Listening to the stories they told, young Alexey was deeply impressed by those men and women who were persecuted as heretics. He admired the strength with which they held fast to their convictions in the face of government authorities who harassed them, imprisoned them, and exiled them to Siberia. But when he thought it over, he realized that their passive tenacity resulted from their inability to get out of their rut and go forward. They clung to old words and outdated dogmas, they were afraid to open their eyes and look at the world. "That faith based on habit is one of the saddest and most harmful things in our life. Like a stone wall, it casts its shadow on everything new, slowing, deforming and weakening its growth."

Living and working among the icon painters eventually became so depressing for Alexey that he felt himself being infected with their sadness and mediocrity. "Boredom weighed down on the workshop, heavy as lead, crushing the men, killing everything in them that was alive, driving them to taverns, or to women who, like vodka, served to make them forget." When he complained of his fate to his grandmother, whom he saw now and then, she sighed and told him to be patient. "But I was not inclined toward patience, and when I practiced that virtue of cattle, trees and stones, it was to test myself, to see how far human persistence could go. Sometimes, out of foolish bravado and jealousy of grown men's strength, adolescent boys try to lift weights too heavy for their muscles and bones. . . . I too did that, both literally and figuratively, and it was only by luck that I did not overstrain and mutilate myself for life. But worse damage is done to human beings by patience and submission to external forces."

At fifteen, tormented by puberty, he was thinking more and more about women. "I had begun wondering if, the next time there was a holiday, I should go where all my companions went. It was not simply a matter of physical desire. I was healthy but I disdained vile pleasures, and sometimes I had a frantic longing to hold someone affectionate and understanding, to talk to her freely about the anguish in my soul, to talk to her for a long time, endlessly, as though to a mother."

In his distress, he thought of going to Persia, probably because he had seen Persian merchants with dyed beards at the Nizhni Novgorod fair, sitting on the ground and staring into the distance as they smoked their hookahs. But he abandoned that plan because of an unexpected meeting: one day during Holy Week, when he was taking a walk, he encountered Sergeyev, his former employer, who was no longer a draftsman and had become a building contractor. He hired Alexey as a watchman at a construction site, with a salary of five rubles a month, plus five kopecks a day for meals.

When the beginning of his job was delayed by a Volga flood, Alexey spent his free time feverishly reading everything he could get his hands on. "I devoured Turgenev and was enchanted by his transparency, his simplicity, his autumnal clarity, the purity of his characters, and the good message he conveyed by describing only what was good." He had less admiration for Dostoyevsky, Gogol, and Tolstoy, yet they also charmed him by the richness of their language. "It was good to read Russian books. Something familiar and sad always came from them, as if there were Lenten bells between their pages; as soon as I opened one of them, the bells rang softly." Sir Walter Scott's novels reminded him of "high mass in a wealthy church: a little long and boring, but always impressive." He was especially fond of Dickens for having mastered "the most difficult artistic achievement: loving mankind."

He became acquainted with some of the high school students who lived nearby and, even though he had a steady and decently paid job, he envied them. He felt that he was freer and more mature than they were, but they had an enormous advantage over him: their formal education. Those cultivated boys talked a great deal about girls, occasionally fell in love with one, and wrote poetry.

At the construction site, Alexey spent most of his time on the lookout for theft, but it took place all around him anyway. The workers stole building materials, tools, and paint. Sergeyev stole trifling objects from buildings to be demolished and took them home. Alexey was repelled by that obsessive greed. "I did not like possessions. I wanted nothing. Even

books seemed to me a hindrance. I had only a little volume of
Béranger, and Heine's lyrics. . . . Furniture, carpets, mirrors
—everything that filled my employer's home displeased me."

During this time he again saw his stepfather, who advised
him on his reading, recommending Goncharov's *Oblomov* and
Flaubert's *The Temptation of Saint Anthony,* a Russian translation of which had just been published in *New Time.* As he
talked with him, Alexey was deeply saddened at the thought
that this prematurely old man, consumed with tuberculosis,
had once been dear to his mother and had insulted and beaten
her. "I knew he was living with a seamstress, and I thought of
her with incredulous pity. How could she not be disgusted at
embracing that long skeleton and kissing that mouth with its
foul-smelling breath? . . . I probably felt no compassion for
him. I saw only one thing: he was dying. . . . Tomorrow he
would vanish, with everything that was hidden in his head
and his heart, with everything I seemed to read in his eyes.
When he was gone, one of the living links that bound me to
the world would be broken."

When his stepfather was about to die, Alexey went to the
hospital to be with him during his last hours. As always in
him, sympathy moderated anger and kindness muzzled revolt.
He later analyzed himself as he was at that time: "I neither
drank nor went with girls; for me, books replaced those two
kinds of intoxication. But the more I read, the harder it was
for me to accept that empty, useless life which, it seemed to
me, was the life that everyone led. . . . I had a strong aversion
to suffering, illness, and injustice. Cruelty—bloodshed,
beatings, even mockery—aroused physical revulsion in
me. . . . There were two people in me. One of them, who had
seen too much baseness and filth, had become mistrustful and
apprehensive, and at the same time he felt helpless pity for
everyone, including himself. He longed for a peaceful, solitary life among books, without neighbors. He dreamed of a
monastery, a forest ranger's cabin, a railroad gatekeeper's hut,

Persia, a night watchman's job out of town, as far away from people as possible. The other one, baptized by the holy spirit of the wise and honest books he had read, realized how easy it was for the overwhelming power of everyday horror to make him lose his head, to crush him under its dirty heel, but he summoned up all his strength and determination to defend himself, clenching his teeth and his fists, always ready for an argument or a fight."

One of those fights broke out because young Alexey had come to the defense of a prostitute mistreated by the doorman of a brothel: "We fought on the ground like two mad dogs. Afterward, sitting in the grass, distraught with inexpressible sadness, I bit my lips to keep from crying. And even now, whenever I remember it I shudder with painful disgust and wonder why I did not become demented and kill someone. . . . The truth is that we all live base and squalid lives. . . . What upset me most was seeing how men treated women. Nourished on novels, I regarded women as the best and most important element in life. I was confirmed in this opinion by my grandmother's stories about the Holy Virgin and the blessed Saint Vassilissa . . . and by having seen the countless looks and smiles with which women, the source of life, give beauty to this existence so lacking in joy and love."

During interruptions of work at the construction site, he had conversations with the laborers, carpenters, masons, and plasterers under his surveillance. "A young cat has been brought in to keep an eye on old rats," they said. These men were all peasants who, when their contracts expired, would go back to their villages and wait to be hired again. From contact with them, Alexey learned to know the mentality of the muzhiks (Russian peasants) and saw that they were quite different from the image of them given by writers. "In books, all muzhiks were unhappy; whether good or bad, they were all poorer in thoughts and words than the muzhiks around me. The muzhik in literature talks little about God, sects, and the

Church, and more about the authorities, the land, justice, and the difficulties of life. He also talks less about women than the real muzhik, and he talks about them with less crudeness and more sympathy. For the real muzhik, women are a pastime, but a dangerous pastime: he must always be crafty with them, otherwise they will get the better of him and throw his whole life into disorder. The muzhik in books is either good or bad, but entirely one or the other, whereas living muzhiks are neither good nor bad, but interesting. The living muzhik may confide many things to you, but you always feel that he is holding something back, and that what matters most may be precisely what he does not say, what he hides."

Alexey was surprised to hear one of those "living muzhiks" maintain that serfdom, which had been abolished nearly a quarter of a century earlier, had had certain advantages for the peasants. "In the days of serfdom, things went better," he said. "The lord was protected by the muzhik, and the muzhik by the lord, and they both lived well and in peace. Noblemen have nothing to gain if the muzhik is poor; they like him to be rich, but he mustn't be intelligent. . . . They say noblemen are a different breed from muzhiks. That's not true. We're the same breed they are, but we're the opposite of them. The nobleman learns from books, of course, and we learn in the fields, and the nobleman has a white ass—that's the whole difference. . . . We're all equal before God."

In these words there was so much ancestral resignation mingled with yearning for a better future that Alexey wondered if the peasants would ever be capable of uniting to struggle against the injustice of their condition. He preferred real workers, prepared to make demands, to these seasonal employees who were still too strongly attached to their plots of land, their village traditions, and their respect for uniforms and cassocks.

Living with muzhiks at the construction site all through the week, he gave himself a change on Sundays by going for a stroll in the poorest part of town. There, on what was ironically nicknamed Millionaires' Street, lived the *bossiaks* (tramps). Alexey was attracted to those derelicts because of their insolence, their gaiety, and their pride in being beggars. He felt that, having no ties, work, or obligations, they had an enviable position in a society of slaves. "They were detached from ordinary life and seemed to have created a joyful life of their own, independent of employers. Carefree and adventurous, they reminded me of my grandfather's stories about Volga barge haulers who readily turned into bandits or hermits. When they were out of work, they did not mind stealing from barges and steamboats. That did not bother me; I saw that life was held together by theft, like an old coat held together by gray thread."

Sometimes it seemed to Alexey that the whole world said to him, "Be a thief. It's no less interesting than being a hero, and it's much more lucrative." He was increasingly repelled, however, by robbery, vulgarity, and violence. The world was repugnant to him. He wanted to escape from it. But how? "I had a strong urge to give the earth and myself a good kick, so that everyone, including me, would begin whirling in a joyful dance, and people would love each other, and a brave, beautiful, honest new life would begin. And I thought, 'I must make something of myself, or I'm lost.'"

He was sixteen at the time of this crisis. Feeling completely isolated, he did not know whom to ask for advice. Nikolai Evreinov, one of his student friends, told him that with his great aptitude for learning he ought to go to Kazan, do some serious studying there, and try to get into the university.

Alexey eagerly accepted this idea. Why hadn't he thought of it himself? For someone like him, there was salvation only in books. In the fall of 1884 he said good-bye to his grandmother. Controlling her sorrow, she gave him one last recommendation: "Don't get angry with people. You're always losing your temper; you've become hard and arrogant. You take after your grandfather! But look what it brought him: all those years of living, just to become a fool and a bitter old man."[2]

Standing at the bow of the steamboat that was about to head down the Volga and take him to Kazan, Alexey saw the stooped figure of his grandmother on the dock. She crossed herself with one hand, and with the other she wiped tears from her cheeks with one corner of her threadbare shawl.

4

STUDENTS

Having arrived in Kazan with his pockets empty of money and his head full of plans, Alexey accepted the hospitality of his friend Nikolai Evreinov, who had urged him to come there and try his luck. The Evreinov family, consisting of a widow and her two sons, lived on her pension in a squalid little house. They barely had enough to eat, and their poverty made Alexey suffer at the thought of being an added burden to them. "And, of course, every piece of bread given to me fell on my soul like a stone."[1]

Naïvely, he still hoped that within a year he could earn a "certificate of maturity" that would enable him to enroll in the university and pursue his studies there, with a scholarship. Nikolai Evreinov tried to improve his friend's education by teaching him, in bits and pieces, everything he remembered from his own reading. "I listened eagerly," wrote Gorky, "but Foucault, La Rochefoucauld, and La Rochejaquelein merged into a single person in my mind, and I could never remember whether Lavoisier had cut off Dumouriez's head or vice versa."

It quickly became obvious to him that he lacked the basic knowledge he would need in order to assimilate all the riches of a university education. Furthermore, living at the expense of that poor and generous family was making him feel increasingly guilty. Finally he stopped taking his meals with the Evreinovs and began leaving the house every morning at dawn. Sheltered in the cellar of a ruined house in the middle of a vacant lot, he watched the comings and goings of stray dogs and wondered if he should not have gone to Persia. "That memorable cellar was one of my universities." But he did not lose courage. "The harder things were for me, the stronger and even wiser I felt. I soon realized that man is created through resistance to his environment."

To keep from starving, he went to the docks of the Volga in search of odd jobs. There he again found himself among dockers, tramps, and thieves, with whom he felt "like a piece of iron plunged into glowing embers." He liked the mocking vulgarity of those men, their primitive instincts, their contempt of the world and its conventions, their unconcern with the future. "Everything I had lived through attracted me to those people and made me want to immerse myself in their corrosive society," he wrote. And: "At times of hunger, rancor, and anxiety, I felt perfectly capable of committing a crime, and not only against 'the sacred institution of property.'" If he did not give in to the temptation of theft and violence, it was because he still had a remnant of childish purity and a vague, romantic desire for excellence inspired by the books he had read. One day a receiver of stolen goods said to him, "Don't get into the habit of stealing, Peshkov. You have a different road to follow. You're an idealist." And when Alexey asked him what an idealist was, he answered, "It's someone who has no envy, only curiosity."

Soon, giving up his dream of higher education, Alexey left the Evreinovs and went to live with another student, named

Pletnev, who advised him to lower his ambition and begin preparing to take an examination that would enable him to become a rural schoolteacher. Pletnev worked at night as a newspaper proofreader for eleven kopecks a day, and if Alexey did not bring in any money the two friends had to be satisfied with a little bread and sugar to ward off their hunger.

Fatigue, anxiety about tomorrow, and lack of food had not put Alexey in a studious frame of mind. He had great difficulty learning what he needed to know for the examination. He was especially repelled by grammar with "its strange, narrow, rigid forms." He could not make "the lively, difficult and capriciously supple Russian language" fit into those forms. And so he was relieved when he learned that even if he passed the examination he could not get a position as a schoolteacher because he was still too young.

Having only one bed between them, the two friends took turns sleeping in it—Alexey at night, Pletnev during the day. This bed was in the hall that served as their bedroom, under a staircase leading to the attic. At the other end of the hall was a table and a chair. The house, half fallen into ruin, sheltered a strange little population composed of starving students, seamstresses, prostitutes, and men "emptied by life," like the tubercular mathematician who chewed his nails till his fingers bled and claimed to demonstrate the existence of God on the basis of pure mathematics. Alexey had great fondness for those disoriented people, as if he already sensed that they would later provide him with the material of his stories and plays.

Among the heterogeneous members of the colony living in the old house were young men who were active in politics and belonged to secret organizations. Attracted to them, Alexey did a few favors for them and was soon admitted into a clandestine "study group" in which a book by Adam Smith was being earnestly discussed. But he was unprepared for theoretical arguments and felt only boredom beneath that avalanche of "long words." With the supercilious pride of a self-educated man, he considered that he had no need to study economic principles because he had "learned them directly" by "expending his strength" and they were "engraved in his flesh."

To those meetings where young intellectuals talked with each other about the suffering of the people, he preferred being with the people themselves—in this case the dockers and drifters who unloaded barges. When, like them, he carried hundred-pound bags, his soul was illuminated by "the almost insane rapture of work." Looking at his fellow workers, he felt like "hugging and kissing those two-legged animals, so intelligent and highly skilled, intoxicated with labor to the point of forgetting themselves." And what a pleasure it was when the owner of the cargo gave them a bonus of "three pailfuls of vodka!"

After a plunge into the dockers' joyous inferno, Alexey came back to the students with the feeling of having used action to make up for the shortcomings of his thought. Moving back and forth between the world of work and the world of culture both exhausted and enriched him. The circle of his comrades was widening from day to day. Whether they were enrolled in the university, the veterinary school, or the Orthodox theological seminary, they all had the same mad desire to change the world. When they had become convinced that Alexey could be trusted, they introduced him to a grocer named Derevenkov, who had a collection of "illegal books" in the backroom of his shop: clandestine publications, articles cut out of revolutionary newspapers, works copied out by hand in school notebooks. In that "library" there were discussions in which Alexey was proud to take part, even though he did not always agree with the impassioned speeches he heard.

Without daring to say it openly, he inwardly reproached those intellectuals for idealizing the people who, "according to them, were the incarnation of wisdom, spiritual beauty, and good heartedness," for bowing to the wretched, ignorant crowd and forgetting that their education and political understanding placed them far above the herd. Knowing the common people—carpenters, dockers, masons, tramps, thieves—very well, he had been able to observe that they had no desire to elevate themselves morally, and not even any love for their fellow human beings. What needed to be done, in his opinion, was to educate them, not to worship them; to draw them out of their squalor, not to celebrate their supposed virtues.

Yet he was moved by his companions' innocent faith. They reminded him of the Old Believers on the banks of the Volga, who tirelessly read large pious books. Like those religious visionaries, the students had noble and illusory convictions. When he listened to them, Alexey felt like "a prisoner promised his freedom." And they looked at him with a kind of professional interest, "as a cabinetmaker looks at a piece of wood from which he can make an unusual object." "A self-taught man," they said to each other knowingly, "a son of the people." He was a little annoyed by their affectionate condescension, and felt that they kept him in the group only because they were curious about the manifestations of his unpolished intelligence.

To make a living, Alexey went to work as an apprentice at a big bakery in Kazan. The kneading troughs and ovens were in the basement. Enclosed in that hot, noisy room, he felt as if he were cut off from the outside world. The sun shone for others. The feet of the people walking past were higher than his head. He worked fourteen hours a day and was then too tired to go to Derevenkov's backroom to meet with the talkative students. Even on his days off he either slept or, lethargic and at loose ends, stayed with the forty other employees of the bakery.

Most of them got drunk to pass the time, and some of them staggered to brothels. Alexey was revolted by their sneering contempt of women. Although he sometimes went with them on their outings, he refrained from having relations with the prostitutes, who made fun of his shyness. As for his companions, after crudely boasting of their sexual exploits they told him they were bothered by his presence, as if they had come to the whorehouse with their father or a priest. He regretted still being a virgin at the age of eighteen, but he could not bring himself to go to bed with one of those homely, foul-mouthed, venal women with whom the customers of brothels were satisfied. When he looked at himself in a mirror he found himself ugly. He disliked his face, with its "high Mongol cheekbones" and his long, ungainly body. Even his voice displeased him.

Meanwhile, Derevenkov had decided to open a bakery, and he asked Alexey to work for him as an assistant baker. Going from one basement to another that was smaller and cleaner gave Alexey the illusion of rising to a higher level of culture. Coming back to Derevenkov, he also came back to the students and again began meeting with clandestine "study groups." Most of the intellectuals he encountered in those groups were *narodniks* (populists) who advocated an idealistic socialism inspired by the ancestral wisdom of the Russian peasant. But among them there were already a few Marxist Social Democrats who advocated direct action and union of the workers. This way of thinking was better suited to Alexey's rebellious temperament. All at once he abandoned lofty dreams in favor of a realistic view of the struggle against the bourgeoisie, czarism, and capitalism.

He felt as if he had been "gripped by an icy wind" when a letter from one of his cousins told him that his grandmother had died. Her funeral had taken place seven weeks earlier; no one had seen fit to notify him at the time. She had fallen and broken her leg while begging in front of a church, and because she was not given proper care, gangrene had set in soon afterward. Now that he had been left alone, without his favorite victim, her husband did nothing but sigh and weep. Alexey thought back over all the happy times he had known with her in his childhood. His last affectionate link with the world had been broken. He wished he could be close to a woman—not to go to bed with her, but to bask in her gentleness, purity, and understanding. "I needed feminine affection, or at least the friendly attention of a woman; I needed to talk openheartedly, to find my bearings in the midst of my disorderly thoughts and chaotic feelings."

For a time he thought he was in love with his employer's sister, Maria Derevenkov. She had a "delicate, tremulous" voice, a pale face, and blue eyes that "looked straight into your soul." But she was obviously in love with a red-haired student and ignored Alexey's sighs. "I tried to imagine her on my lap, but I felt in my whole being that it was impossible, and the idea frightened me." One day, watching him carry heavy bags of flour, she said to him, "You've got enough strength for three men, but you're clumsy. Even though you're tall and lanky, you're a real bull!"

He agreed that his excessive vigor made him clumsy. Even in discussions with his friends, he spoke in a heavy, violent way. He was a hybrid, both a worker and a poet. He had recently begun writing poetry, but he was able to express himself only in highly individual terms, "in my 'own' words," as he put it. A student said to him, "You don't use words when you talk—you use iron weights!"

He was so tormented by the contradictions in his character that he did not know who he was, to what social category he belonged, or what he expected of the future. "Everything attracted me: women and books, workers and carefree students. But I did not succeed in being anywhere; I lived with neither the workers nor the students. I was spinning like a top, while a strong unknown hand vigorously lashed me with an invisible whip."

In early December 1887, disoriented and exasperated, Alexey decided to kill himself. He was nineteen. With the money he had saved up, he bought an old army pistol. Then on December 12, at eight o'clock in the evening, with the feeling that he was about to end an absurd situation, he went to the bank of the Kazanka River and shot himself in the chest. In one of his pockets the police found an ironical note: "Please hold the German poet Heine responsible for my death: he invented toothache of the heart. Herewith you will find my identity papers, which I have had drawn up specially for this occasion. I ask that my body be dissected and examined, to find out what kind of devil has been living in me lately. The passport included herewith will show that I am Alexey Peshkov, and I hope that this note will show nothing at all."

Luckily the bullet missed his heart; it went through his left lung and lodged in his back. He was quickly taken to a hospital, where his condition was judged to be so serious that the surgeon, Dr. Plushkov, hesitated a long time before deciding to operate. The operation succeeded beyond all expectation. But Alexey made another suicide attempt, this time by swallowing some hydrochloride that was in a bottle near his bed. His stomach was washed out and he regained consciousness. Some of his friends came to see him in the hospital. One of them scornfully called him a fool.

With his robust constitution, Alexey was able to get out of bed in five days, and not long afterward he went back to work at the bakery. Now that he had miraculously escaped death, he was ashamed of having tried to kill himself. He saw that desperate act as a failure to cope with the difficulties of life, a kind of cowardice unworthy of someone determined to fight for freedom. Meanwhile, the suspicious police had given his suicide note to the local consistory of the Orthodox Church for a more thorough study of the Peshkov case. The priest of his parish, Father Malov, sent him two summonses, which he ignored. Then the consistory ordered him to come to the Saint Theodore Monastery to be questioned about the reasons for his suicide attempt and instructed on the meaning and purpose of earthly life.

The ecclesiastical tribunal before which he appeared was composed of a monk, a priest, and a professor from the Kazan Theological Academy. Facing those eminent spiritual judges, he refused to give any explanation of his "atheistic act" and, defying their authority and mocking their dogmas, he said that he regarded himself as the only rightful master of his life and his soul. They sentenced him to seven years of excommunication.

This sentence left him indifferent. Without openly denying the existence of God, he had long since turned away from the official church.

5

PEASANTS

In March 1888, soon after Alexey had resumed his work at the bakery, a friend of Derevenkov's named Mikhail Romass came to see him and offered him a job in the shop he had opened in the large village of Krasnodivovo, about twenty-seven miles down the Volga.

Romass, a massive giant with a light brown beard and thick crewcut hair, was a moderate populist belonging to the clandestine group known as the People's Right (*Narodnoye Pravo*). Whereas members of the People's Will (*Narodnaya Volya*) engaged in terrorist action, those of the People's Right felt that by educating the peasants they could succeed, without bloodshed, in transforming the empire into a happy democracy in which all officials, from the humblest to the most prestigious, would be elected by universal suffrage. But even this peaceful doctrine was not to the liking of the authorities. Accused of subversive activities, Romass had been exiled to Yakutsk for ten years. He had returned only in 1885. His long

stay in Siberia had not made him change his views. He was
more firmly convinced than ever that he was in possession of
the truth.

He promised Alexey easy work, plenty of free time, and
access to all sorts of illegal books. His plan was to win the
peasants' trust by selling them merchandise more cheaply
than other shops and, when he had drawn them to him in this
way, awaken them to progressive political ideas. The hot-
headed young Alexey, whom he had been able to observe in
Derevenkov's bakery, would be of great help to him in that
propaganda enterprise.

Alexey gladly accepted his offer, and two days later he took
a steamboat for the trip down the Volga to Krasnodivovo.

On the evening of his arrival, he had a conversation with
Romass that was to stay in his memory. "You're gifted,
strong-minded, and obviously full of good intentions," Romass told him. "You should be learning, but in such a way
that books won't cut you off from people. . . . We must say to
the peasant, 'You're not too bad a man, but your life is bad
and you don't know how to make it better and easier. . . .
Everything came from you, the peasant. Noblemen, priests,
scholars, czars—they all used to be peasants. . . . Learn how
to live so that you won't be beaten any more.'" Alexey listened to these artless words with pleasure. They taught him
nothing new, but the trust and warmth he sensed in them
opened up such prospects of friendship that he was exhilarated. "He talked to me a long time, till midnight," he wrote
in *My Universities*, "with an obvious desire to put me on the
same level as himself. For the first time, I felt truly at ease
with another human being. My self-esteem had been considerably lower since my suicide attempt; I felt diminished and
guilty, I was ashamed to be alive. Romass must have realized
this. Simply and humanely, he opened the door of his life to
me and helped me to regain my pride."

To win Alexey over completely, Romass showed him his
library, in which there were not only Locke, Taylor, Mill,

Darwin, and Spencer, but also Goncharov, Nekrasov, and Pushkin. With his broad hand he affectionately stroked the volumes "like kittens."

More and more strongly attracted to books, Alexey did not understand how Romass could show the same fondness for humble people as for great minds. He himself was excited by the works of poets and philosophers and could only condemn the narrow, spiteful mentality of the peasants. He found them more backward than the workers in towns and cities. Exhausted by work that was almost beyond human strength, they knew nothing of gaiety and joking, and lived "as if they were blind"; they were constantly afraid of disaster, complained all day long, and mistrusted each other "like wolves." Arguments and fights broke out among them over nothing. Because of a broken twelve-kopeck pot, three families fought each other with clubs, and when it was over, an old woman had a broken arm and a young man with a fractured skull was bleeding heavily. From morning till night, the women whined about their ailments. The young men of the village pursued them with revolting shamelessness. They would catch one of them in a field, pull up her skirts, leaving her naked from the waist down, and tie them over her head. This was called "turning her into a flower." The women were not particularly offended by it, and protested only for the sake of form. "I did not like the country," wrote Gorky, "and the peasants were incomprehensible to me."

Alexey confided his disappointment to Romass, who tried to explain to him that the peasants' depravity and brutishness were perfectly understandable in people who had been freed from serfdom only twenty-seven years earlier. Unable to get used to their new condition, they were still czarists at heart. They felt that it was "bad to have many masters, and better to have only one." And, trusting in the wisdom of their "little father," the czar, they waited for the day when he would proclaim "true liberation" and "sharing for everyone." Then, they believed, everyone would seize the piece of land he had been coveting. Meanwhile, as they lived in expectation of that universal brawl, they stayed on their guard, kept an eye on each other, exchanged hatred for hatred, and "sharpened their teeth." According to Romass, this turn of mind that flourished in the Russian countryside had to be taken into account by anyone who wanted to approach the peasants, reassure them, and open their eyes.

Despite the efforts of Romass and Alexey, however, the villagers remained hostile to them. The very fact that Romass sold them merchandise more cheaply than anyone else, and defended them against the scheming of usurers and newly rich peasants, seemed suspicious to them. The leading citizens of Krasnodivovo banded together to intimidate the socialist shopkeeper, talked with the poor people he wanted to help, and turned them against him. Strangers shot at him and Alexey; one of his most loyal supporters was murdered with an axe; and in August 1888, his house and storage shed were set afire. Charred bits of paper floated in the smoke. "My poor books!" Romass lamented. "I loved them so much!"

When Alexey, horrified, began reviling the criminals who had started the fire, the gentle Romass said to him, "You're angry with the peasants? You shouldn't be. Their malice is only foolishness." But Alexey rejected that saintly resignation. "I don't know how to live with such people," he replied. "I *can't* live with them!" He had come to hate the whole village. No doubt about it, the peasants could not be counted on to make the revolution. Only the workers were worthy of taking part in the final battle.

Accepting defeat in Krasnodivovo, Romass decided to leave and preach the good word somewhere else. He had not given up hope for peaceful change. "Don't be in such a hurry to condemn people..." he said to Alexey. "Look around you calmly and remember this: everything ends, and everything changes for the better. Slowly? Yes, but lastingly."

After Romass had left, Alexey felt "leaden distress," as he described it. He wandered from village to village "like a puppy that had lost its master." Finally he decided to leave that unfriendly region. He and a young peasant named Barinov went to work on a barge heading down the Volga. But at Simbirsk (now Ulyanovsk) the crew put them ashore because they found their attitude suspicious. They had only thirty-seven kopecks in their pockets. Their aim was to reach the Caspian Sea. They stowed away on a passenger train that took them to Samara. There they again got work as barge hands. A week later they arrived at Astrakhan and went to work in a Kalmuck fishery. Soon afterward, Alexey set off by himself, intending to walk to the Caucasus. He wandered here and there, doing odd jobs to earn his living. Early in 1889 he returned to the banks of the Volga, the river that had fascinated him since his childhood, and began living in Tsaritsyn (later Stalingrad, now Volgograd).

This city, like several others on the Volga, was one of the places where the government kept political agitators in forced residence. Some were merely suspected of subversive propaganda; others had returned from exile in Siberia and were still forbidden to go to any of the large university cities. Since most of them were intellectuals, they easily found work in railroad administration. One of those unrepentant "progressives" took an interest in Alexey and got him a job as a night watchman at the Dobrinka station. Armed with a club, Alexey walked around the warehouses from six in the evening till six in the morning. Theoretically, he was supposed to keep thieves away, but he knew that the stationmaster had a nearby shop in which he sold tea, flour, and sugar stolen from freight cars.

He was surrounded by ugliness, deceit, and coarseness. Every Saturday the schoolteacher beat his wife in the bathhouse; she would then come running out, naked and screaming, and he would run after her with wooden rods in his hand. There were orgies in which men drunk on vodka undressed women to feel their breasts and bellies, and one of these men once cried out in front of Alexey, "Brothers, look at me! I don't have a human face!" The police chief's cook put some of her menstrual blood into the cookies she gave to a railroad engineer to arouse his "tender feelings." A little later, having learned of this witchcraft, the engineer hanged himself in his cellar. "After everything I had seen," Gorky wrote in *My Universities*, "the lives of the sedate intellectuals seemed to me colorless and boring, far removed from the dark, stupid agitation that made up everyday life. I had the impression that those intellectuals were unaware of their isolation in that dirty little city where everyone was alien and hostile to them, where people cared nothing about Mikahilovsky[1] or Spencer and had no interest at all in the importance of the individual in the historical process." More than ever, he saw a great gulf between "bespectacled bookworms," draped in "a mantle of erudite words," and the crude, uncultivated mass of the people, moved by bestial instincts. "There is a profound difference between them, almost a racial difference."

After making his nocturnal rounds, he was often ordered to clean the stationmaster's kitchen, sweep the bedrooms, cut firewood, wash dishes, or take care of the horse. Exasperated at having to do this extra work, he sent an ironic letter to the head of the district that included the Dobrinka station: "I continue to live properly and I have become friends with my colleagues [the other watchmen]; I have a clear understanding of my duties and I perform them scrupulously. The stationmaster is satisfied with me and, to show that he trusts me and is favorably disposed toward me, he tells me every morning to take the garbage out of his kitchen. Please let me know if cleaning the stationmaster's kitchen is one of my obligations."

This was followed by a satirical letter on the same theme, but written in verse. It caused laughter in high places and its author was transferred to the Borisoglebsk station, where he was responsible for guarding and maintaining the brooms, sacks, and tarpaulins. These new duties left him more time for reading. "I avidly yearned to commune with that beauty which allures us so much in books, and to find a love that would strengthen me. More and more often I felt surges of hot, dark anger rising in me, blinding my reason, turning my concern for people into heavy disgust."

Since his conduct was irreproachable, he was soon given a job with more responsibility: he became the "weigher"—that is, the employee in charge of the scales—at the Krutaya station, eight miles from Tsaritsyn. Shortly after his arrival there, he organized a "study group" composed of himself and four other people: two telegraphers, a locksmith, and a printer. Unlike the students and intellectuals in Kazan, the members of the new group were simple, self-taught men who complained about their situations in life but did not believe that a social upheaval was imminent.

The police quickly got wind of their secret meetings. Afraid of being arrested, they began wondering if, instead of dreaming of revolution, they might not do better to listen to Tolstoy, who was preaching a return to the land and the creation of "free rural communities." Maybe that faraway prophetic writer really had the keys to wisdom, justice, and happiness. They sent him a collective letter, signed "Alexey": "It is said that you own much uncultivated land. We therefore ask you to give us a piece of it." The letter was never answered.

Not at all discouraged, Alexey decided to go and see Tolstoy in Moscow, to ask him for help and advice. In May 1889, he left Tsaritsyn with his inflamed mind full of daydreams about an independent life without bosses, among good friends, on land that he would plow and sow himself, to produce crops that he would harvest himself. He made that very long trip partly on foot and partly in freight trains, traveling at night with the crew in the brake van. In his bag, along with his spare clothes, he had a poem "in prose and verse," "The Song of the Ancient Oak," which he had written passionately, throwing into it "all the ideas I had gathered during the past ten years of my hard and varied life." He hoped to show this first effort to Tolstoy.

But he did not find the writer at his country estate, Yasnaya

Polyana, or at his house in the suburbs of Moscow. There, however, he was able to meet Tolstoy's wife. She was coming out of a hut full of books. Before he could explain the reason for his visit, she told him that her husband had gone off on foot to the Troitz-Sergeivsk monastery. Since Alexey seemed tired, she took him into the kitchen and graciously gave him a roll and coffee. Then she casually mentioned that "shifty loafers" came to see Tolstoy, and remarked that Russia was heavily infested with such parasites. "I had already noticed it myself," Gorky wrote in *My Universities*, "and I was able to agree with that shrewd woman's observation politely and without hypocrisy."

Disappointed but with his pride intact, Alexey resigned himself to going back to his beloved Volga. This time he chose his hometown of Nizhni Novgorod. Since he was now without a kopeck in his pocket, he persuaded a trainman to let him get into a cattle car. For thirty-four hours he traveled with eight head of hobbled cattle that snorted, lowed, and stamped their feet in dung and urine. By the time he reached his destination he felt as if he were one of them, ready for the slaughterhouse.

6

FIRST LOVE

Nizhni Novgorod was teeming with political offenders in forced residence. In 1888 and 1889, that revolutionary brotherhood had been enlarged by an influx of students expelled from Kazan after the university disturbances of 1887. Among them Alexey found two of his old comrades: Chekin, a former schoolteacher from Kazan, who had been dismissed because of his subversive opinions, and Somov, a former exile. They invited him to live with them in a little house on Zukovsky Street. Mitzkevich, a Marxist sympathizer who met Alexey at this time, later wrote in his memoirs, "Before me stood a tall, long-haired young man wearing blue glasses, a black shirt, an overcoat, and boots." Chekin introduced him: "This is Peshkov, an interesting man; he comes from the people."

Being political offenders, Chekin and Somov were, of course, spied on by the police, and their house was kept under discreet surveillance. Since he lived with them, it was inevitable that Alexey would also be suspected by the authorities. He behaved irreproachably, however, and earned his living by working in the basement of a beer warehouse. The political police in Nizhni Novgorod asked for reports on him from Tsaritsyn and Kazan, but the information they received did not enable them to accuse him of being involved in any plot.

It was not until October 1889 that the net tightened around him. A clandestine printshop was discovered in Kazan, and orders came to Nizhni Novgorod from St. Petersburg to arrest Somov as a presumed accomplice of the printers. On October 12, the three friends' house was searched and Alexey was interrogated. According to the official police report, he answered questions "with effrontery and even insolence." He was imprisoned in Nizhni Novgorod and released soon afterward because examination of the papers, books, and photographs seized in his home had not revealed anything conclusive.

General Poznansky, head of the secret police, was in charge of the investigation. He sent the records of it to the governor of Nizhni Novgorod with these comments: "The answer that I received from the chief of police in Kazan, in response to my request for information on Peshkov, confirmed me in the opinion I had already formed, namely, that Peshkov offers fertile ground for the activities of questionable people in Russia. That answer informed me that Peshkov had worked in a Kazan bakery organized with subversive intentions, that in that city he had relations with suspect individuals, and that he read tendentious, undesirable books not in keeping with his intellectual level or his education." In conclusion, General Poznansky recommended keeping Peshkov under "secret and discreet surveillance." A similar report was sent to St. Petersburg.

While Alexey was celebrating his release with some of his friends, a former exile, Sabunaev, of the People's Will, said to him pompously, "Prison is an indispensable school for a revolutionary." Alexey judged him to be ridiculously affected and answered him curtly.

He happily accepted an offer to work as a clerk for a liberal lawyer named Lanin, who took an interest in the case of that "young outlaw" with a thirst for literature. Meanwhile, the military authorities tried to draft Alexey into the army, but he was declared unfit for service because of his "punctured lung." For once he was glad of his suicide attempt.

He had not forgotten his poem, "The Song of the Ancient Oak." Not having been able to show it to Tolstoy, he decided to show it to another writer, Korolenko, who lived in Nizhni Novgorod. Korolenko was a former political exile and the author of several stories that were very popular at the time. He was shoveling snow in front of his house when Alexey introduced himself to him. "Good-natured bluish eyes looked at me above a fringe of curly whiskers enriched with frost," wrote Gorky. Leaning on his shovel, Korolenko listened to the newcomer explain the reasons for his visit, then took him into a little room cluttered with books and began reading the manuscript. Now and then he stopped to reproach the young author for misspelling or misusing a word, needlessly using foreign words, or resorting to coarse expressions to convey the strength of his feelings. Beneath this barrage of criticisms, Alexey reddened "like a burning coal." He was sorry he had come and wanted only to run away and hide his shame.

When he was back home, he thought with despair about the ruin of his literary ambitions. "I resolved to write nothing more, neither poetry nor prose, and I kept that resolution during the whole time of my stay in Nizhni, about two years. With great sorrow I sacrificed the fruit of my wisdom to the purification of fire."

For a time he thought that frequenting intellectual circles would console him for his failure. But discussions between "populists" and "radicals" interested him less and less. His comrades seemed to him "heroicomic" in their misinterpretation of the spirit of the masses. "I saw that they painted the people in colors that were too delicate," he wrote in *My Universities*. "I knew that the 'people' they talked about did not exist on earth. On earth, the grasping, crafty, short-sighted little peasant lived patiently, looking with suspicion and hostility at everything that did not concern his self-interest. The thickheaded little townsman also lived there, packed full of superstitions and prejudices even more venomous than those of the peasant; and the hairy, powerful merchant, deliberately and legally organizing his savage life." In his distress, he again thought of killing himself. "My soul was very sick. If my personal experience two years earlier had not convinced me that suicide was stupid and humiliating, I would certainly have used that cure." He also thought of other kinds of violence: "I felt capable of committing a crime out of curiosity; I was ready to kill, just to find out what would happen afterward."

A short time later, with the same exuberance, he forgot about his metaphysical anguish and fell in love with a married woman ten years his senior: Olga Kaminsky, who had returned to Russia after living in Paris among the émigrés and was the mother of a charming four-year-old girl. Alexey was probably no longer a virgin by this time, but what did his sordid debauchery with venal women amount to, compared with the glorious desire that now possessed him? "It was terribly painful for me to restrain that passion: it consumed me and physically exhausted me. It would have been better for me to be simpler and more direct, but I believed that relations between a man and a woman should not be limited to that physiological union whose wretched coarseness and animal simplicity I had come to know. The thought of that act was almost repugnant to me, even though I was a vigorous, rather sensual young man with an easily excitable imagination."[1] To his astonishment, the "lady of his heart" told him that she loved him as he loved her. His passion immediately flared up and he asked her to share his life. With delicate charm she called him a madman, put forward the age difference between them, spoke of how desperate her husband would be if she left him, and finally, advised Alexey not to try to see her again.

"Half sick and close to insanity," he decided he had to get away from the city, the woman he desired in vain, the revolutionary intellectuals whose endless discussions disappointed him, and his whole past, with its series of failures in love, writing, and politics. He felt that only a long period of aimless wandering across Russia could cleanse his soul of the mud that had accumulated on it since his birth. Now, at the age of twenty-three, he had a stronger need than ever before to see, absorb, and understand the Russian people—not the Russian people in books, but those who labored and suffered in the land of their ancestors. In April 1891, he packed some of his belongings into an oilskin bag and left Nizhni Novgorod on foot to discover *his* country, *his* brothers, *his* vocation.

7

MAXIM GORKY

When Alexey left the city, warm spring sunshine was melting patches of snow in the fields near the river. The road was muddy. He walked along the right bank of the Volga, looking back occasionally to see if he was being followed by a police spy. But evidently no one cared about his departure. Farther on, he took a boat to Tsaritsyn. From there he went by train to Filonovo, where he joined his friend Yurin, a telegrapher and former member of the "study group" with which he had hoped to create a Tolstoyan "free rural community." Yurin took him into his home and introduced him into his new group of friends, who were more radical than his old ones.

Alexey was again plunged into an atmosphere of verbiage and feverish excitement. The local police knew about the group's secret meetings. From an official report of May 29, 1891: "While maintaining surveillance of railroad employees, in accordance with paragraph thirteen of instructions to the police, we noticed some time ago that several young men had begun meeting in the home of the supervisor of the Filinovo station, the technician Chichagov, originally from the town of Borisoglebsk. The young men are: Yurin, a telegrapher, of peasant origin; Khlebnikov, a technician in the repair shop; Frolov, a schoolteacher in the hamlet of Berezovsky; and Alexey Maximovich Peshkov... from Nizhni Novgorod, temporarily residing in Filonovo. All the above-named persons meet in Chichagov's home, and the meetings usually last until midnight or even later. They always have the curtains drawn and the doors locked, so that no one can look inside or come in unexpectedly. In view of the secretive character of the above-named individuals, and their suspicious conduct, there is good reason to assume that illicit schemes against the authorities are elaborated during their meetings. It may also be assumed that the above-named individuals are in possession of harmful and prohibited books, because they generally see to it that no one outside their group can read them."

In spite of these specific suspicions, the police took no action against the little group and Alexey was able to leave Filinovo, in search of a peace that still eluded him. "I was living in a thick fog of contradictory thoughts, desires, and feelings. I needed to find in life and people something that could lighten the weight crushing my heart."

He tirelessly walked to the Don steppes, then to the fields of the Ukraine, and finally to the Black Sea region, stopping here and there along the way to earn a few kopecks and rest awhile. On July 15, 1891, he was going through a large village near Nikolayev when he saw a peasant tormenting his unfaithful wife in the midst of a laughing, jeering mob. The poor woman, half naked, was hitched to a wagon and the peasant was whipping her to make her pull it. Alexey tried to intervene, but the onlookers attacked him and threw him unconscious into the bushes. An organ-grinder on his way back from a fair put him into his cart and took him to a hospital in Nikolayev. Alexey stayed there till he recovered, then resumed his journey. He worked with some Black Sea fishermen, took a job in a saltworks, harvested grapes in Bessarabia, worked as a docker in Odessa, and continued traveling, still on foot, till he reached the Crimea and the territory of the Kuban Cossacks.

When he came into Maikop, the town was in turmoil. An epizootic disease had killed many of the cattle in the surrounding pastures, and the authorities had then given the absurd order to put all the remaining animals into a single enclosure, which made it certain that the sick ones would transmit the disease to the others. The infuriated Cossacks had driven the sanitary commission out of town. To restore calm, a company of riflemen and a detachment of dragoons were sent in. Three rebels were hanged as a warning to the others. On September 18, 1891, the inhabitants of their village held a funeral service for them. This displeased the authorities: they saw it as an act of provocation against the government. Alexey, who happened to be passing by at the time, joined the crowd and was arrested and imprisoned. A copy of the New Testament was found in his bag and, strangely, this made the police think he was a religious fanatic preaching rebellion to the rural population. The policeman in charge of his interrogation asked him why he had been wandering all over the country. "I want to know Russia," Alexey answered. "This isn't Russia," the policeman said contemptuously, "it's a pigsty."

Released a few days later, Alexey resumed his random wandering. He walked along the northern range of the Caucasus Mountains toward the Caspian Sea, then turned back and walked toward the Black Sea. He then headed into the mountains, and at Vladikavkaz he took the Georgian military road to Tiflis (now Tbilisi).[1] He made part of the journey with a young Georgian who claimed to be a prince. An idler, a liar, and a coward, this strange companion lived at Alexey's expense, sometimes even stole from him, and slipped away at the slightest danger. When they arrived in Tiflis, he told

Alexey that he had rich relatives there who would be glad to give them food and lodging. Then, claiming to have an errand that would take only a few minutes, he left him in the street and disappeared into the crowd.

It was late October and very cold. For six hours, shivering and cursing, Alexey vainly waited for his companion to come back. Finally he went into a tavern to get warm. Some drunks greeted him with jeering remarks. A fight broke out and the whole group was taken to the police station. So the dirty walls of a jail cell formed the setting of Alexey's first night into the Caucasian capital. He was in danger of being charged with "suspicious vagrancy" and sent back to Nizhni Novgorod, his "legal domicile," after staying in several other jails along the way. But in the course of his interrogation he was able to give a reference: a man named Nachalov, who lived in Tiflis and had been his superior when he was a railroad employee at Dobrinka and Krutaya. Because of this, he was released the next day.

Nachalov himself had advanced social ideas. He offered to find work for Alexey and let him stay in his room. Employed in the administration of the Transcaucasian railroad, he got his protégé a job in the ironworks, then in an office. He also introduced him into the intellectual circles of Tiflis, composed of political offenders in forced residence.

Alexey soon left Nachalov's room and moved in with a worker named Afanasiev. Other young revolutionaries joined them. Their community became a center of attraction for manual laborers, students at the Pedagogic Institute and the seminary, women schoolteachers, apprentice midwives. Referring to his stay in Tiflis, Alexey wrote to a friend, "I read books with students from the institute and the seminary. I don't teach them anything, I only advise them to understand each other. I also talk with workers from the railroad depot. There is a worker here named Bogatyrovich. He has a good disposition and I get along perfectly with him. He says there is nothing good in life and I tell him that what is good is hidden so that the first bastard who comes along can't get his paws on it."

In the midst of all that bustle and agitation, he tried to organize his time systematically: from nine o'clock in the morning till four in the afternoon, work; from four to five, his evening meal; from five to nine at night, reading; from nine to eleven, political discussions; from midnight to three or four in the morning, writing and more reading. Yes, he was now writing again, having forgotten his angry decision to give it up forever.

He was encouraged in his writing by Alexander Kaliuzhny, a wise populist who had spent several years in prison and was now living in Tiflis in forced residence. That grave and affectionate man had a beneficial influence on him. He tried to calm his youthful excitement and make him think about using his talent as a storyteller. Thirty-four years later, Gorky wrote to him to thank him for his understanding: "My dear friend, my teacher. . . . Since I met you, I have known hundreds of people, some of them important and remarkable. But, believe me, none of them has been able to efface your image in my heart. You were the first to look at me with your kind, friendly eyes, not as a strapping young man with a strange biography, a useless vagabond, amusing but suspect. . . . I immediately realized that I must not brag about anything in front of you, and it seems to me that, thanks to you, I have never bragged in my life. I have never exaggerated my self-esteem or the misfortunes that life has abundantly dealt me."

Kaliuzhny listened delightedly when Alexey told about the ups and downs of his nomadic life, and he advised him to write down whatever came into his mind. Alexey wrote a story entitled "Makar Chudra" and read it to his friend. Charmed by the folkloric originality of its subject and the romantic richness of its style, Kaliuzhny took it to the editor of the local newspaper, the *Caucasus*. But Alexey had very little hope of its being published; without waiting for an answer from the newspaper, he set off on another journey in the summer of 1892. He crossed Georgia, went down to the Black Sea, and worked on building a road from Sukhum (Sukhumi) to Novorossisk.

When he came back to Tiflis, he was amazed and delighted to learn that the *Caucasus* had accepted his story. Still doubting his good luck, he hurried to the offices of the paper for confirmation. There, a journalist asked him what name he wanted to use for his first published piece of writing. Alexey hesitated; his real name, Peshkov, suggested the idea of abasement and humility to him, since the Russian word *peshka* means "pawn." He was anything but a pawn in the human throng. He remembered that because of his "sharp tongue" his father had been nicknamed Bitter, *gorky* in Russian. That would be a wonderful pseudonym for a young writer rebelling against society. So he chose Gorky, "Bitter," as his last name, and Maxim as his first. On September 12, 1892, the *Caucasus* published "Makar Chudra," by Maxim Gorky, a newcomer in the world of writing.

Another joy soon followed for Gorky: finally divorced from her husband, Olga Kaminsky came to join him in Tiflis, with her daughter. At their first meeting he nearly fainted from emotion. "She seemed to me even prettier and more charming," he wrote in *My Universities*. "She still had her girlish figure, her cheeks had kept their rosy tint, and her cornflower-blue eyes their tender glow. . . . I wanted to die and, so to speak, breathe her into my soul, so that she would stay there forever." He read his story, "Makar Chudra," to her and she listened with a mixture of affection and gracious condescension.

Paralyzed with love, not daring to kiss her or even touch her, he said in a faltering voice, "Come and live with me. Please. Let's live together." She went to one corner of the room and answered from there, smiling, "Here's what we'll do: you'll go to Nizhni Novgorod and I'll stay here, think it over, and write to you." He bowed to her respectfully, "like the hero of a novel I had read," and went away, walking on air. Soon afterward, in accordance with Olga's wishes, he went to the shore of the Caspian Sea, boarded a sailing ship, and went up the Volga to Nizhni Novgorod.

8
JOURNALIST

Gorky reached Nizhni Novgorod in October 1892, and was immediately hired again by Lanin, the lawyer. Olga and her daughter arrived a little later. She and Gorky rented a bathhouse from a priest for two rubles a month and the three of them settled into it as best they could.

But Olga soon proved to be shallow and coquettish. She liked to admire herself naked in a mirror and stir up Gorky's jealousy by accepting attentions from other men. He called her "a bonbon"; liked her "odor of bitter almonds"; appreciated her gaiety, her carefree attitude, and her aversion to domestic quarrels; but regretted that she was not more interested in literature. Once when he was reading one of his stories to her, she fell asleep, with her breathing "as calm and even as a child's. I thought that story would appeal to women and make them hunger for freedom and beauty," he wrote in *My Universities*, "but the woman closest to me was unmoved by it, and had fallen asleep. Why? Was the bell that life had put into my chest not resonant enough? I had taken that woman into my heart in place of a mother. I had hoped she would nourish me with intoxicating honey, stimulate my creative powers, and soften the harshness I had acquired on the roads of life." As one disappointment followed another, his feelings for Olga cooled; he had placed her too high in his esteem.

His work for the lawyer consisted of copying writs of summons, complaints and appeals, written in a jargon that irritated him. Between incursions into the world of legal wrangling, he delivered himself from boredom by writing stories and poems. But although he read them to Olga and a few close friends, he did not have enough confidence in them to submit them to the local newspapers. One of his friends "borrowed" a manuscript from him and sent it, unknown to him, to *Russian News*, an important Moscow daily. Against all expectation, the story ("Emilian Pilai") was accepted and Gorky was proud to know that an important newspaper of the liberal opposition, whose usual writers were professors and famous authors, appreciated his prose.

In "Emilian Pilai," the character of the tramp, so close to Gorky's heart, makes his first appearance. "What is my life?" he asks. "A dog's life. But I have no kennel and no food. . . . Am I a man? No, brother, I'm worse than an earthworm, worse than an animal. Who can understand me? Nobody!"

Encouraged by this initial success, Gorky sent several stories to a newspaper in Kazan, the *Volga Herald*. The editor accepted them and published them with flattering comments. One of the stories, "Of the Siskin Who Lied, and the Woodpecker, Lover of Truth," is resolutely symbolic and full of implications. In it the siskin, who represents revolutionary fervor, invites the other birds to fly off to "the land of miracles and happiness," beyond the forest. But the woodpecker, who "lives on earthworms," denounces that illusion and, sticking to the facts, convinces his companions that no such paradise exists. Finally the siskin has to admit that he lied "because it is good to hope and believe." Young intellectuals recognized themselves in the optimistic siskin, condemned the sensible woodpecker, and agreed in praising the vitality of the author's thought.

Korolenko read this allegory soon after returning from a trip to the United States. He asked Gorky to come and see him and, with his usual frankness, gave him some helpful advice. Though he recognized his young colleague's narrative talent, he urged him to give up verbiage, redundancy, and flashy effects. This amounted to asking Gorky not to be himself. He was incapable of concision and, it seemed, selectivity. His writing was a torrent whose violence and richness surprised him as much as anyone else. And his vision of the world corresponded to his own character: frank, direct, guileless, and passionate. There were the good and the wicked, heroes and scoundrels, tormentors and victims. No subtle shadings, no concessions. Absolute darkness or dazzling light. Chiaroscuro was banished from art. Writing consisted in smiting demons and exalting angels. But while he excelled in depicting negative characters, his positive characters were rather pale and conventional. Korolenko had seen this from the start, and he often told Gorky, "Don't embellish people." He also insisted that Gorky should work more on his style and write a longer story, intended not for a newspaper, but for a magazine.

Gorky followed his advice and wrote a story, "Chelkash," which Korolenko judged to be excellent. "Your characters talk and act by themselves, according to their temperament," he told him. "You don't interject yourself into their thoughts and feelings, and that's something not everyone can do. . . . I've already told you that you're a realist. . . . But at the same time you're a romantic."

After this success, Korolenko put Gorky in touch with a large newspaper in Samara, which hired him as a columnist at a salary of a hundred rubles a month. But to take that job, Gorky had to leave Nizhni Novgorod and go to live in Samara. He did not hesitate a second. His relations with Olga had become bittersweet. She was indifferent to his two passions, literature and politics, and she was behaving in a ridiculously maternal way toward a student who wrote poetry for her. In Gorky's eyes, "the fairy" was gradually losing all her charm. He felt affection and compassion for her, but the essential fire had gone out. He told her that he thought he should go away and she agreed that it would be best for them to separate. "After a sad silence, we embraced strongly and I left town. . . . So ends the story of my first love, a happy story in spite of its bad ending."

He arrived in Samara on February 23, 1895, and went to work the next day. He wrote a daily column on local matters for the *Samara Gazette*. Because censorship was very strict, he had to be satisfied with writing about such things as incidents in the street, a performance at the Samara theater, a visit to the town by a traveling menagerie, the bad behavior shown by certain young men in public, the way patients were treated in the municipal hospital, or the harm done by prostitution. But even in those mild articles his tone was harsh. Some readers recognized themselves in his attacks on the bourgeoisie or businessmen, and complained to the paper's management. On Sundays he published a literary feature, either a story or a poem. In one of his poems, "Farewell," he expressed his disappointment following his breakup with Olga:

> Love is always a little deceitful,
> Truth always struggles with it,
> We wait long for a woman worthy of it,
> We wait in vain, and then we take
> Meat wrapped in rags for a good fairy.
> Farewell!

Meanwhile, his success with the public and within the newspaper business was growing steadily. Early in 1896 he was hired as an editor by a large new paper in Nizhni Novgorod, the *Nizhni Novgorod Leaf*, and he happily left Samara to return to his hometown. Another large provincial paper, the *Odessa News*, asked him to be its special correspondent at the Pan-Russian Exposition opening that year in Nizhni Novgorod.

His work for both papers keenly interested him from the start. He now had a much broader field of investigation than he had had in Samara. The government wanted the "industrial and artistic" exposition to illustrate the development of Russia in the last years of the nineteenth century. As a showcase of capitalist success, it was sure to displease Gorky. "This exposition is, of course, highly valuable to merchants and manufacturers," he wrote in one of his articles, "but it tires people and arouses too many bitter thoughts in them." Wandering among the gaudy, ornate pavilions, listening to the exclamations of the crowd, and attending the receptions of Pan-Russian associations in his capacity as a reporter, he developed a real hatred of the well-to-do, whose main concerns were money and ostentation. Even the liberal bourgeoisie, who claimed to care about the happiness of the people, seemed suspect to him. Although he belonged to no revolutionary organization, he considered that leftist intellectuals who talked instead of acting were tarred with the same brush as thoroughgoing conservatives. He felt visceral hostility against anyone who did not come from the lower levels of society.

The more he saw of the exposition, the more its glitter seemed to him an insult to the misery of the poor, and he was galled at not being able to say so in his articles. Now and then, however, he slipped a few caustic words into one of them. "The people do not come to the exposition," he wrote. "The public can be seen there. But is the public the people?

The people, as always, are busy with their own affairs, and have neither the money nor the time to come and see the wonders of Russian industry."

Having to supply hastily written copy to two daily newspapers at once, Gorky soon came to feel that this heavy labor was beyond his strength. Since his suicide attempt, his lungs had been the weak point of his body. Doctors discovered that he had incipient tuberculosis and advised him to go to the Crimea, the Russian equivalent of the Riviera, for treatment. But he lived entirely on his income as a journalist and had no savings. His friends helped him to apply for money from the St. Petersburg Literary Fund, an organization for assisting needy writers and scholars. The required formalities proved to be long and complicated.

In the meantime, a stroke of luck had brightened Gorky's life. At the offices of the *Samara Gazette* he had met Ekaterina Pavlovna Volzhin, a young woman of eighteen who had recently been hired as a proofreader. She was the daughter of a former landowner who, after being ruined, had become an estate steward. Pretty, vivacious, cheerful, and modest, she was attracted to Gorky at first sight. She herself was an ardent revolutionary. As she listened to him telling about his adventurous life, she wanted to become better acquainted with this violent and tender man who had primitive instincts and spoke so well. She was also impressed by the care with which he corrected the proofs of his articles and his kindness to the workers in the print shop.

To celebrate the new year of 1896, the newspaper gave a costume party. Gorky came to it dressed as a tramp. It ended at six in the morning. As he was taking Ekaterina home, he abruptly asked her to marry him. She said yes, with no hesitation. But her worried parents begged her to wait. They felt she was too young and they were dismayed by Gorky's tumultuous past. Furthermore, they said, she had a good education, having finished high school with a gold medal, whereas he was a self-taught man of extremely humble origin. But then her father died, her mother gave in, and the wedding took place discreetly in Samara in August 1896.

Before deciding on their future, the young couple had to wait for the Literary Fund to answer Gorky's request. The money finally came at the beginning of 1897. They were overjoyed to get it and immediately left for the Crimea.

There, Dr. Alexin treated Gorky and restored him to good health. In the spring of that same year the couple went to stay at the estate of a friend of Ekaterina's, Manuilovka, in the government of Poltava. Still convalescing, Gorky spent much of his time talking with the peasants of the nearby village and was soon on close terms with them. He organized an amateur theatrical group for them and, in their log huts, they made costumes and painted sets. He was both the state manager and an actor in the improvised performances.

On July 27, 1897, Ekaterina gave birth to a baby boy who was named Maxim and affectionately called Max. Gorky was elated. It seemed to him that becoming a father had redoubled his creative powers. When autumn came, he decided to go back to Nizhni Novgorod and continue working as a journalist. He was now sure of his vocation and he had a lofty idea of what it meant to be a writer. He felt that anyone lucky enough to have a talent for writing should place it in the service of a noble cause. He should not write to amuse himself or others, but to denounce the flaws of society and urge the common people to improve their lives. Art and utility were inseparable. The man of letters was not an entertainer, but a guide.

When he left the Ukrainian village where he had finished his convalescence, the grateful peasants wanted to go with him to the railroad station about eight miles away, but they had drunk so much vodka to drown the sorrow of parting that most of them collapsed on the roadside, dead drunk.

9

THE STORMY PETREL

Gorky had scarcely settled down in Nizhni Novgorod when the police came to arrest him. His photograph, with a friendly dedication written on it, had been found in the home of Afanasiev, a worker with whom he had spent a great deal of time in Tiflis in 1892. Afanasiev himself had just been imprisoned for "distribution of illegal publications." Despite the flimsiness of the charges against him, Gorky's home was thoroughly searched, and he was sent to Tiflis under escort for further questioning. The police brought a sealed package containing the "evidence": more than five hundred letters, notes, and manuscripts.

Gorky arrived in Tiflis on May 11, 1898, and was put into a cell in the Metekh castle. A police report said of him, "He is an extremely suspect man; literate and a good writer, he has traveled over most of Russia (and usually on foot)." A witness declared that, having met Peshkov in 1892, he had been "struck by his politically untrustworthy behavior," and that he "often talked violently about the exploitation of workers by their bosses."

These allegations were not enough to indict Gorky, because they were related to his stay in Tiflis in 1892, whereas the revolutionary organization created by Afanasiev dated only from 1897. He was released after two weeks of detention. But even though nothing incriminating had been found in the papers seized in his home, the police ordered that he be kept under even stricter surveillance. From now on, he could not travel or change his residence without permission from the police, and if he obtained that permission he had to go to his destination by an approved route and was not allowed to stop along the way, "except in case of illness or circumstances beyond his control." In the latter case, he was required to notify the local police immediately.

From Tiflis he went to Samara to invigorate himself by taking a course of treatment with kumiss (fermented mare's milk, which was believed to be a tonic). Then, in August, he went back to Nizhni Novgorod, where his wife and son were waiting for him. He was in a cheerful mood despite his trouble with the police—by now, he was used to being plagued by them. And his career as a writer was off to a good start. His first book, *Sketches and Stories*, had just been published in Moscow. Getting it into print had not been simple. One publisher rejected the manuscript because, he said, a distinguished firm like his could not let itself be associated with stories that had appeared in provincial newspapers. The next publisher to whom Gorky submitted the manuscript decided to take it, but was so unsure of his decision that he asked him to write a preface to justify the book in the eyes of the critics and the public. "I regret not being able to give you the preface you want," Gorky replied, "but . . . I am incapable of writing it. I tried, and it gave the impression that I was defiantly shaking my fist at someone, or that I had committed a sin and was tearfully repenting of it. Since neither of those impressions suits me, I gave up the attempt." The publisher dropped his request for a preface.

The book was published in two volumes, each containing about ten stories. The first printing of three thousand copies sold out so quickly that the publisher and the author were both surprised. The fresh, harsh, biting tone of the stories roused the public from a kind of elegant apathy. Since the deaths of Dostoyevsky (in 1881) and Turgenev (in 1883), Tolstoy had been towering over the Russian literary landscape. He preached submission to God outside of the Church, nonviolence, and reliance on the ancestral wisdom of the peasant, who embodied all the virtues of the Russian race. Beside him was Chekhov, who, with extraordinarily delicate brush strokes, depicted the tedium of everyday life in the provinces and the pangs of conscience suffered by irresolute intellectuals. But newcomers were already rebelling against the "social" literature, preferring free, individualistic, and artistic writing situated beyond good and evil. This was the school of decadent symbolists: Sologub, Briusov, Balmont, Merezhkovsky.

Above this chorus of morbid whisperings, Gorky's voice suddenly rang out like a bugle call. In the crude, blunt language of his stories, he attacked the petty bourgeois mentality and extolled the merits of popular anarchy. His ragged tramps and vagabonds were contrasted with the ignorant, crafty peasant as well as the rich landlord. He shouldered his way past defenders of the peasantry, portrayers of stay-at-home reality, and amoral esthetes. Young Russian intellectuals had been impatiently waiting for a champion of revolt against the established order. Glutted with humanitarian theories and subtle refinements, they were thirsty, to use Chekhov's expression, for "something tart and bitter." Gorky came at just the right time to satisfy those protesters in search of a leader. A man from the lower classes, dressed as a worker, he shouted and

swore, and that violence pleasantly jolted the nerves of a de-
caying society. He was showered with praise.

Even more than his stories, it was his prose poems that won
favor with intellectuals yearning for acton. In one of those
poems, "Song of the Falcon," he glorified the "madness" of
the falcon, who rose into the air, attacked the enemy, and
died a victim of his own courage, whereas the snake, crawling
on the ground, denounced the illusion of those whose supreme
goal was to reach the sky. Another of his prose poems, "The
Stormy Petrel," celebrated the sea bird flying above the foamy
waves and hurling into the storm a cry that expresses "the
power of anger, the flame of passion, and the certainty of
victory," while the pigeons, never having known the joy of
combat, tremble at every thunderclap. In Gorky's story "Old
Woman Isergil," Danko, a hero of the struggle for freedom,
tries to lead the members of his tribe in search of justice and
light, and when they refuse to follow him, he tears open his
chest with his bare hands, takes out his flaming heart and
holds it above his head to light the way.

The naiveté of these allegories and the heaviness of their
style might have made readers smile, but their ideological
content won the approval of young people eager for exploits
and outbursts. The refrain of "The Stormy Petrel"— "We glorify the madness of the brave!" —became the revolutionaries'
slogan. Gorky's bombastic poem was circulated in hundreds
of printed, typewritten, and hectographed copies, and it was
written out by hand in clandestine groups of workers and students.

After a period of calm, many of those young people had
come back to the tradition of the People's Will. They dreamed
of plots, decisive actions, heroic sacrifices that would bring
on the downfall of the loathsome czarist regime. Some of them
joined the Socialist Revolutionary Party. From there, the most
resolute and "capable" went into the terrorist groups that
stalked the czar's grand dukes, ministers, and high officials.

Those specialists in political assassination often claimed kinship with Danko, the man who sacrificed himself by tearing out his heart to light the way for his brothers in misfortune.

Others, however, hostile to the doctrines of the People's Will, were drawn to Marxism and Social Democracy, which had only recently come into existence and was steadily gaining ground among the intelligentsia. These were revolutionaries of a different type: they mistrusted the peasants, whom they considered to be narrow-minded, greedy, and czarists at heart, and felt that they could rely only on the urban proletariat to destroy the old order. Only enlightened workers, used to group living and therefore receptive to propaganda, could help the intellectuals seize power. So when Gorky denounced the peasants' innate flaws, he became the idol of the Social Democrats; and when he condemned the degradation of a Russian society that lacked ideals, he was regarded as a champion of the Socialist Revolutionaries. All those who proclaimed the need for drastic change in Russia recognized themselves in him and sang his praises. Unknown only a short time before, he now appeared as the man who articulated the demand for justice.

Encouraged by the success of his stories and prose poems, he wrote to his publisher in a letter dated April 19, 1898, "The way the public has received my works strengthens my conviction that I will soon be able to write something really good. I have begun a thing in which I place great hope because with it I intend to awaken shame in people's hearts."

The "thing," on which he worked all winter, was his first novel, *Foma Gordeyev.* In it he depicted the world of merchants and industrialists in Nizhni Novgorod, as he had known it when he was reporting on the exposition in 1896. Although he recognized the energy of those rich capitalists, he stigmatized their greed, their selfishness, their contempt for the work of others, and their domineering spirit. Foma Gordeyev, the brutal, ignorant son of one of those cruel magnates, feels a kind of metaphysical despair over the emptiness of his life. He plunges into coarse orgies in an effort to "forget himself," but they fail to soothe his torment. He then causes a scandalous disturbance at an official banquet by hurling abuse at the leading citizens of the city. After this outburst against the Russian bourgeoisie, he is declared insane and placed in an asylum. He finishes his life as a visionary beggar wandering along the roads in search of truth. Reflecting on himself, he says, "A man goes down a river in a boat. . . . The boat may be strong, but under it the water is deep. . . . If the man begins feeling that dark depth, no boat will save him." Foma Gordeyev perishes because under his feet he feels the "dark depths" of the capitalist world.

This time, Gorky included quibbling intellectuals in his contempt for the bourgeoisie. "I wish," says one of his characters, "that I could gather the scraps of my poisoned soul and spit them, with my heart's blood, into the faces of our intellectuals, may the devil take them! I'd say to them, 'You cost our country so much, you foul lice, and what do you do for it? You reason too much! Your hearts are full of morality and good intentions, but they're lukewarm and soft, like an eiderdown quilt!'"

By condemning the intellectual elite in this way, Gorky was detaching himself to some extent from the Socialist Revolutionaries, who considered that the intellectuals, far from being harmful phrasemongers, were the main means of awakening the masses, and he was moving closer to Marxist Social Democrats, who felt that the revolution would be brought about entirely by the industrial proletariat. As a self-taught man, he could not cure himself of his inferiority complex with regard to "pseudoscholars," and he centered all his hopes on the workers, with whom he had a visceral feeling of solidarity. Like the Marxists of that time, he believed that the liberation of the workers would have to be accomplished by the workers themselves, and that intellectuals were there only to comment and applaud.

But revolutionaries were not the only ones who appreciated

Gorky's writing. He also had bourgeois admirers who relished his fresh violence. Rich and protected, they felt a delightful thrill of novelty when they met the tramps, hoodlums, and anarchists he brought into their living rooms. He and his books became the latest fad. Even the great writers of the period regarded him as one of them. *Foma Gordeyev* was published in 1899 in the St. Petersburg newspaper *Life*. Its edition in book form was dedicated to Chekhov. Gorky had corresponded with him when his *Sketches and Stories* was published. In sending him a copy of it on October 24, 1898, Gorky had written, "The truth is that I would like to confess the warm, sincere, unrequited love I have had for you since my early youth. I have spent so many divine moments in the company of your books, I have so often wept as I read them, so often rebelled like a wolf caught in a trap, so often laughed for a long time!" And in another letter, dated December 6, 1898, "I do not know how to express my admiration of you; I find no words for it, and I am sincere, believe me."

Without ever having met Chekhov, Gorky revered in him the artist who could depict a state of mind or a landscape with the simplest words, and also the man who denounced the lack of vitality in most of his contemporaries. It seemed to him that he and that painter of everyday dullness were going in the same direction. But Chekhov only pointed up the vices, absurdities, and boredom of a decadent society, whereas Gorky wanted to use his whole mind and all his muscles to help tear down the rotten structure.

In corresponding with Chekhov, Gorky hoped to learn from him the magic secret of his art. And Chekhov gently, patiently, and frankly advised his young colleague from a distance. As Korolenko had done earlier, he criticized Gorky for his lack of restraint, his wild verbiage, and his taste for rare adjectives. "Your lack of restraint appears mainly in the descriptions of nature that you intersperse with dialogue passages," he wrote to him on December 3, 1898. "When I read those descriptions, I wish they were shorter and more compact, only two or three lines. The frequent references to voluptuousness, whisperings, velvety softness, etc., give the descriptions a tinge of rhetoric and monotony. They chill and tire the reader. Your lack of restraint is also evident in your portraits of women."

Far from being offended by such criticism, Gorky accepted it gratefully. "What you say about my rare words is true and fair," he wrote to Chekhov in December 1898. "I have not been able to banish them from my vocabulary; also, my fear of being crude prevents me from doing it. . . . I am self-taught." And, in January 1899, "You said that I am intelligent, and I laughed. I am stupid as a locomotive. I have been on my own since the age of ten, I have never had the means to get an education, I have done nothing but devour life and work, and life has warmed me with its blows." Finally, in a letter written on April 22, 1899, he made this candid request: "To put it plainly, I beg you not to forget me. I would like you to point out my faults now and then, give me advice and, in general, treat me as a comrade who needs to be educated."

When he had read *Foma Gordeyev*, however, Chekhov did not have the heart to tell Gorky how disappointed he was. He confided his real feelings about the book to Posse, editor of the newspaper *Life*, in a letter dated February 29, 1900: "*Foma Gordeyev* is as monotonous as a dissertation. All the characters have the same way of talking, and they also think in the same way. They do not speak spontaneously, but for a purpose. They all seem to have mental reservations; they do not express themselves completely, but as if they still had something at the back of their mind. Actually, though, they have nothing more: it is only their way of talking."

Chekhov had liked the free, spontaneous tone of Gorky's stories and he was now worried by the new didactic orientation that had appeared in *Foma Gordeyev*. He felt that a novelist should "show" and not "demonstrate," that his characters should have a life of their own in the midst of their contradictions, rather than being illustrations of a general

idea; and that their story should produce emotion, not conviction. In short, he was against "commitment" in literature, and
he sensed that Gorky was more and more strongly attracted to
fiction with a "message." To Chekhov, writing meant painting;
to Gorky, it meant proving.

They must have had occasion to compare their opposing
views when Gorky went to Yalta, where Chekhov was staying,
in March 1899. Here they finally met in person, and they
liked each other from the start. Chekhov appreciated the
blunt sincerity and explosive idealism of that writer who had
sprung from the people. "He has the appearance of a tramp,"
he wrote to Lydia Avilova on March 23, "but inwardly he is a
very elegant man." And on March 30, in a letter to Rozanov,
"I have been seeing Gorky, the writer, here. He is a simple
man, a vagabond, who did not begin writing until he was an
adult. As if he were benefiting from a second birth, he now
enthusiastically seizes anything in print and reads it openheartedly, without prejudices."

As for Gorky, he was captivated by the modesty, lucidity,
and manly gentleness of that very great writer who treated him
as an equal. "Chekhov is a remarkable man," he wrote to his
wife on March 22. "People are mad about him and won't leave
him in peace. . . . Conversation with him is delightful, and I
can't remember ever getting such pleasure from talking with
anyone else." Gorky, who wanted so much to devote himself
to a cause, learned from that discreet, dignified, self-assured
man, who looked like a provincial schoolteacher, that one
could be good-hearted without belonging to a party, and want
to improve the people's lot without dreaming of bloody battles.

But while he admired the independence of Chekhov's
mind, he was unable to go against the demands of his own
nature, which was violent and unbridled, in love as well as in
anger. After leaving Chekhov he wrote to him, on April 23,
"It seems to me that, of all the men I have known, you are the
only free man who bows to nothing. It is good that you can see
literature as the first, most important concern of life. As for

me, though I feel that it is good, I am probably not capable of living as you do. I have too many other likes and dislikes. I regret it, but I can do nothing about it."

Toward the end of 1899, Gorky's popularity reached proportions that amazed him. Even though he had still not published very much, symposiums on his work were held in St. Petersburg and a portrait of him by Repin became the chief attraction of a mobile exhibition. It was mainly young people who gathered before the picture of their new idol. In Nizhni Novgorod, his apartment served as a meeting place for lovers of literature and devotees of politics. He collected money to send poor children to school, worked to create a home for the destitute, and organized charity festivals to provide Christmas trees and presents for the needy.

He was kept under constant surveillance, exercised by either uniformed policemen or plainclothes agents of the Okhrana, the czarist secret police. One of those agents, named Ratayev, wrote in his report, "Subversive activity in Nizhni Novgorod, which had completely died down before the exposition, is again in full swing, and everyone here who has revolutionary tendencies lives and breathes only through Gorky." Another agent wrote, "Peshkov [Gorky]" cleverly combines legal activities (publications, participation in authorized works of charity) with clandestine activities, and he thus transforms lawful enterprises into revolutionary ones."

Irritated by this spying, Gorky wrote to Chekhov in September 1899, "Lately I have been as ill-tempered as an old witch. My mood is dark. My back and my chest hurt, and my head does its part too. . . . Under the influence of my gloominess, I have begun drinking vodka, and even writing poetry. I feel that a writer's trade is not pleasant." And in January 1900, "Our time yearns for heroism. Everyone wants something exciting and spectacular, something that is not like life, but is loftier, better, and more beautiful. It is essential for current literature to embellish life a little, and as soon as it begins doing so life will seem more beautiful and people more high-spirited and animated. But look at them now—what ugly eyes they have: boring, listless, and cold!"

In December 1900, as a result of university disturbances in Kiev, 183 students were drafted into the army as privates. When Gorky learned of this, he wrote indignant letters to his friends: "Forcing students into the army is an abomination, a shameless crime against individual freedom, an idiotic measure taken by scoundrels puffed up with power." Some of these letters were intercepted by the police. In defiance of all caution, he went to St. Petersburg. On March 4, 1901, a crowd of students gathered, in front of the Cathedral of Our Lady of Kazan to protest the drafting of their fellow students. Gorky was among the demonstrators. They were brutally charged and dispersed by Cossacks and mounted policemen.

When the government gave a watered-down account of this incident, Gorky signed a protest by intellectuals against repressive violence. The police believed he was the author of a tract entitled *Refutation of the Government's Version*; but they had no proof. A short time later they established that he had donated two thousand rubles to a fund for university agitators. He was also accused of having come to St. Petersburg for the purpose of acquiring a mimeograph machine with which to reproduce subversive pamphlets intended for workers in the industrial suburb of Sormovo. When he returned to Nizhni Novgorod he was imprisoned, then released because of the bad condition of his lungs, but sentenced to confinement in his bedroom. "One policeman was stationed in the kitchen of my apartment," he later wrote, "and another in the antechamber, and I could not go out unless I was escorted by one of them."

That year he had published another novel, *The Three of Them*, which was even more polemical and committed than the one before. Three young men—Lunyev, Grachev, and Filimonov—are trying to find their way in life, each according to his temperament. The only one who succeeds in making his actions conform to his aspirations is Grachev, who joins a political group, steeps himself in socialist ideas, becomes an enlightened worker, and even proves to have a talent for writing poetry.

This novel, intended to prove once again that capitalism was the relentless enemy of the workers, gave Gorky an even greater audience and increased the authorities' mistrust of him. An order was given to send him to Arzamas, a small town near Nizhni Novgorod, but then he had a recurrence of tuberculosis and was told that he could first go to the Crimea to regain his health. Since his train would pass through Moscow, he also obtained permission to stop over there for a week so that he could make personal contact with the Moscow Art Theater, which was going to present his first play, *The Petty Bourgeois*.

The Petty Bourgeois was another attack against the propertied classes, with a family conflict centered on a railroad worker named Nil, who represented "the new man," "the real man," "the exemplary worker." This is how Gorky characterized him in a letter to Stanislavsky, head of the Moscow Art Theater, in January 1902: "A man calmly sure of his strength and his right to rebuild his life according to his own ideas." The fact is that this model of working-class virtue lacked originality and depth, but the play came at a time of grave political tension, and Gorky was convinced that he would be striking a great blow by truthfully depicting a son of the people on the stage. He also knew he would have to fight a long time to get past the barrier of censorship, but he was determined to be patient.

Before leaving for the Crimea via Moscow, he had an unexpected triumph: the liberal intellectuals of Nizhni Novgorod —lawyers, doctors, professors—gave a banquet in his honor to show their indignation at his being sent away by "administrative decision." Some of the city's students decided to attend the banquet to let those advanced bourgeois know that Gorky did not belong to them and that only revolutionary students could claim him. Altogether, about a hundred and fifty people

came. In their speeches, the liberals were vague and grandil-
oquent; the students issued a call to action and struggle.
Gorky responded by reading a pamphlet he had written:
"About a Writer Puffed Up with Vanity." In it he criticized
himself, but also his readers: "It is not good for a writer to
have many admirers. Anyone who has dealings with the public should disinfect the atmosphere with the carbolic acid of
truth." And he attacked liberal intellectuals who wanted "a
warm, peaceful, comfortable life" in an outdated edifice "impregnated with the blood of those who have been crushed by
our society." This "decayed, tottering" edifice needed only a
jolt to make it "come crashing down." "Soon," he prophesied,
"different men will come, bold, honest, strong men—yes,
soon!" These words set off a storm of cheers and protests in
the banquet hall.

Fearing more disturbances, the police hastened Gorky's
departure: he was given an order of immediate expulsion. On
November 7, 1901, hundreds of students carried him in
triumph to the railroad station. They sang, shouted political
slogans, and threw hectographed proclamations into the
crowd: "We are gathered here to accompany our famous and
beloved writer Maxim Gorky, and to express our anger at his
expulsion from his native city. He is being expelled only because he has told the truth and denounced the injustices of
Russian life. . . . We want to fight, and we *will* fight against
this state of things."

Lifted into the train with his wife, his son Max and his
daughter Ekaterina (Katiusha), who was still a baby, Gorky
was embarrassed by this noisy glory. He wondered if he was
worthy of it and tried to reassure himself with the thought that
those demonstrations of enthusiasm were not addressed to his
talent but to the people, whose basic demands he expressed.

Telling about his journey in a letter to Posse later that
month, he wrote, "In the stations, masses of policemen. In
Kharkov I was advised not to leave the train. Even so, I went
out onto the platform. The station was empty. . . . In front of it,

a crowd of students and other people. The police would not let them come any closer. Shouting and commotion—someone had just been arrested, I was told. The train started off. It was one in the morning. A pitch-black night. Suddenly, when Piatnitsky and I were on the platform of the car, in the dark, there was a loud, fierce, belligerent roar. We learned that the iron bridge across the station was full of people shouting and waving their hats; it was a wonderful, brotherly thing to do. The bridge was high above the train and the shouting was so stormy, so friendly, so strong! I am telling you all this, comrade, not to glorify Gorky to you, but to show the mood that is becoming more and more common among the best part of the Russian public."

Worried by these demonstrations, the police withdrew Gorky's permission to stop over for a few days in Moscow. Before the train reached the old city of the czars, his car was separated from it and sent about thirty-two miles away, to the little town of Podolsk, and he was ordered to wait there for a train that would take him to the Crimea. When they learned of this change, the friends who had intended to meet him at the station in Moscow—his publisher, his German translator, the famous singer Chaliapin, the writer Ivan Bunin, and others—took a suburban train to Podolsk. A joyous banquet was improvised under the noses of the furious police. When, late at night, the participants accompanied Gorky back to the station, where the express was to make a special stop for that troublesome traveler, what had begun as a bit of governmental harassment ended as the glorification of a martyr to freedom.

The public liked everything about that man hounded by the authorities: his crude behavior, his black peasant shirt buttoned up the side and held at the waist by a thin leather belt, his thick mustache, his unruly shock of hair, his piercing eyes, his Volga accent, what was known about his vagabond youth, and even the weakness of his lungs, which made him seem a romantic hero from an earlier time. He was thus not only a writer whose stories were held in high regard but also an extraordinary personality, a star of the literary scene. Those who admired him affirmed both their political preferences and their taste for his unpolished, Manichaean writing. Irritating some and exciting others, he left no one indifferent. But that was in keeping with the goal he must have set for himself: to shake up the unconcerned, the undecided, and the timorous, and be "the stormy petrel."

10

THE STAGE

Although he had been given permission to go to the Crimea for his health, Gorky was forbidden to stay in Yalta, the most elegant vacation resort on the coast. Ignoring the prohibition, he stayed for a week in Chekhov's house there. A policeman stood guard in front of the garden gate. Whenever Gorky left the house, the police chief called Chekhov to find out where his undesirable guest had gone.

Gorky then rented a house in Oleiz, not far from Gaspra, and moved into it with his wife and children. He and Chekhov saw each other often and their friendship steadily became warmer. "Alexey Maximovich [Gorky] has not changed," Chekhov wrote to his wife, Olga Knipper, on November 17, 1901. "He is still the same honorable, kind, and intelligent man. There is only one thing wrong in him, or rather on him: his peasant blouse. I can no more get used to it than to a chamberlain's uniform." As for Gorky, he never tired of praising Chekhov's modesty, integrity, and clear-headedness. "I believe," he wrote in his *Reminiscences*, "that with Anton Pavlovich [Chekhov] all visitors felt a desire to be simpler, more sincere; in short, to be more themselves. . . . Chekhov did not care for those conversations on 'lofty subjects' with which Russian men so often like to intoxicate themselves, forgetting that it is ridiculous and stupid to talk about velvet suits in the future when one does not have a decent pair of trousers in the present."

Gorky was all the more deeply moved by his illustrious colleague's graciousness because he knew he was in the final stages of tuberculosis and not expected to live much longer. Bearing his illness with smiling stoicism, Chekhov went on advising Gorky, urging him again and again to avoid verbiage and turgidity in his writing, and gently contradicting him in their political discussions. To that convinced Marxist who wanted a total revolution that would sweep away the bourgeoisie and establish the rule of the proletariat, he tried to set forth the possibility of a less precipitous solution: the slow transformation of the czarist regime into an enlightened liberal one. Despite their difference of opinion on this point, the two men shared a love of humble people and a devotion to literature.

Not far from the Gorkys' house in the Crimea lived Tolstoy. After a serious bout of malaria, his doctors had recommended that he finish his convalescence in the sun of the Black Sea region. He had come in a special railroad car and begun staying at a castle in Gaspra that a friend, Countess Panin, had placed at his disposal. Gorky, who had already met him in Moscow and at Yasnaya Polyana, paid him frequent neighborly visits. Like Chekhov, Tolstoy respected the talent of that young writer who had come from the people, but deplored his grandiloquence. He was especially interested, however, by his roughhewn personality and emphatic ideas.

The two writers, one thirty-three and the other seventy-three, differed in almost every way. Whereas the plebeian Gorky had had a destitute and vagabond youth, the rich and noble Count Leo Tolstoy had spent most of his life in splendid isolation on his estate, totally out of touch with the urban proletariat. Detesting modern mechanization and "the false culture of the intellectual elite," Tolstoy saw salvation only in submission to the ancestral wisdom of the Russian peasant. In his desire for simplification, he condemned pell-mell the doctrine of art for art's sake, the antiquated rites of the Church, and the domination of the individual by the state, and he preached refusing to respond to violence with violence. He felt that this nonresistance, heroic but passive, would lead people to reject all governmental constraints, such as military service, the courts, and administrative decisions, and enable them to live free in the delights of brotherhood.

This utopian vision of the future was alien to Gorky: he was close to the workers, hostile to the peasants, an advocate of direct action, and an implacable enemy of Christian resignation. The first time he saw Tolstoy, he was touched by his friendly welcome but thought he could discern in it the condescension of a great nobleman who, to put his lowborn guest at ease, talked to him in a falsely folksy manner. Later, recalling those fascinating encounters, Gorky wrote with rare perspicacity, "Tolstoy's peasant beard, his rough but extraordinary hands, his very simple clothes—that whole democratic exterior misled his visitors, and I occasionally saw some of my compatriots, used to judging people by their way of dressing (an old serf habit!), begin to take with him that tone of malodorous candor which is more specifically called familiarity. . . . And suddenly the old Russian nobleman, the magnificent aristocrat, would come out from behind the facade of the peasant beard and the wrinkled blouse, and the familiar visitor would then feel a chill run up his spine. At those times it was pleasing to observe the nobility and grace of his gestures, the discretion of his speech, and the delicate precision of his murderous words."

Actually, neither Tolstoy nor Gorky was at ease in that confrontation between two social classes. The count, who tried to look and act like a peasant, dreaded the mocking expression of his visitor, who had really known poverty; and with each word, Gorky felt the intellectual superiority of his host disguised as a peasant. "His interest in me is ethnographic," Gorky wrote in his notebook. "To him, I am a member of a little-known tribe, and nothing more." And, noting that Tolstoy had irritably said, "I'm more a peasant than you are, and I feel more as a peasant does," Gorky commented, "Oh, God, he mustn't brag of that, no, he mustn't!" Though they were always on the alert with each other, the two men enjoyed having rambling conversations about literature, music, the theater, politics, God. Tolstoy questioned Gorky on his reading; demonstrated that his thinking on literature was "puerile", denigrated Victor Hugo, "the bawler", and declared, "The French have three writers: Stendhal, Balzac, and Flaubert. Maybe Maupassant can be added to the list, but Chekhov is better. As for the Goncourt brothers, they were clowns; they only pretended to be serious. They studied life in other people's books."

One evening he surprised Gorky by asking him bluntly, "Why don't you believe in God?"

"I don't have faith."

"That's not true; you're a believer by nature and you can't do without God. If you don't believe, it's out of stubbornness, and out of resentment that the world isn't as you'd like it to be. . . . Faith, like love, requires courage and temerity. You have to say to yourself, 'I believe,' and then all will be well."

This conversation took place in Tolstoy's study. Sitting cross-legged on his couch, the old master smiled ironically, raised his finger, and said, "You can't evade that question by silence." "And though I don't believe in God," Gorky later wrote, "I looked at him, I don't know why, with great wariness, with a little fear too, I looked at him and I thought, 'This man is like God.'"

But Tolstoy could not convert Gorky to Christianity, any more than Gorky could convert Tolstoy to the religion of rebellion. They agreed only in condemning the doctrine of art for art's sake and maintaining that a writer ought to educate his compatriots. In 1900, Gorky had written to Chekhov, "Leo Tolstoy does not like people, no, he does not. He only judges them cruelly and really too harshly. His idea of God does not appeal to me. Is that a God? It is part of Count Leo Tolstoy, and not God, that God without whom people cannot live. He says he is an anarchist. To some extent he is. But while he destroys some rules, he decrees others that are just as strict for people, and just as burdensome. That is not anarchism; it is the authority of a provincial governor."

Years later, in July 1908, he expressed himself more forcefully in a letter to Vengerov: "Count Leo Tolstoy is an artistic genius, perhaps our Shakespeare. But although I admire him, I do not like him. He is an insincere man: inordinately enamored of himself, he sees and knows nothing except himself. His humility is hypocritical and his desire for suffering is repulsive. Such a desire usually comes from a sick, perverted mind, but in this case the arrogant Tolstoy wants to be put in prison only to strengthen his authority. . . . No, that man is foreign to me in spite of his very great beauty."

While Gorky was still in the Crimea he learned that he had just been elected a member of the Russian Academy of Sciences, in its literary section. When Czar Nicholas II read this in the *Official Monitor* of March 1, 1902, he wrote in the margin, "More than original!" and expressed his disapproval in a letter to the minister of public education. How could a writer with revolutionary tendencies, who was being watched by the police and had spent time in prison, be part of such a respectable assembly? The academy was ordered to cancel that unseemly election. It obeyed.

The effect was the opposite of what the government expected. Because of this interference in the realm of literature, Chekhov and Korolenko—members of the academy—resigned from it out of solidarity with Gorky, who was once again presented as a martyr to freedom of thought. When it was suggested to Tolstoy that he, too, should resign from the academy, he gruffly refused, saying that he did not consider himself a member of it. The fact is that Gorky was glad to be excluded from the company of official celebrities. Anything that could accentuate his image as a rebel was welcome to him.

During the affair of the canceled election to the academy, the affair of *The Petty Bourgeois*, Gorky's first play, also took place. Permission to perform it was refused, then the censors demanded cuts, and Sipiagin, the minister of the interior, sent a letter to Grand Duke Sergey, the governor general of Moscow, to suggest that he appoint an official who would attend the dress rehearsal and report the effect that certain lines produced on the audience. "In this way," he wrote, "we might be able to prevent the public presentation of passages or expressions which, when read to oneself, do not arouse negative feelings, but which spoken on the stage, might produce an undesirable effect." Permission was finally granted, but only for four performances before carefully selected audiences composed entirely of people who had already subscribed to the theater.

The management of the Moscow Art Theater decided to give the first performance in St. Petersburg, during a tour, on March 19, 1902. But the authorities demanded a special dress rehearsal. Nemirovich-Danchenko, codirector, with Stanislavsky, of the Art Theater, later described what happened: "Fashionable society was informed with incredible rapidity and we were overwhelmed with requests for seats and boxes from the families of high government officials and the diplomatic corps. The play attracted a distinguished, elegant, politically influential audience that would not have been out of place at a European congress." The theater was surrounded by large contingents of policemen, on foot and on horseback. As a precautionary measure, the ushers were replaced by policemen. The St. Petersburg opening was followed by the

Moscow opening, but in neither city did the long-winded, doctrinaire play achieve the success expected of it.

Undiscouraged, Gorky continued working on another play that he had already begun: *The Lower Depths*. After a restful stay in the Crimea he had gone to Arzamas, which had been designated as his place of forced residence. Relegated to that sleepy, dusty little town with unpaved streets and wooden sidewalks, he had lost none of his fiery spirit. His new play, finished in a few weeks, was a masterpiece of vividness and violence. By evoking the atmosphere of a shelter for the homeless, with its human wreckage—false intellectuals, fallen noblemen, derelicts, drunkards—it offered a microcosm of all the passions and miseries of a rotten society.

At the end of August he obtained permission to go back and live in Nizhni Novgorod; and on September 5, 1902, he was in Moscow, reading *The Lower Depths* to the actors of the Art Theater. They were overwhelmed by that descent into hell. When one of them asked him what effect he wanted to produce on the public, he answered, "I'll be satisfied if you can shake the audience so much that they can't sit comfortably in their seats."

A censor's certificate was needed. At first it was refused. Nemirovich-Danchenko went to St. Petersburg to try to get it and had to do battle with acrimonious censors over every sentence and word. Finally, permission to perform the play was granted for a simple reason: after the poor showing of *The Petty Bourgeois*, the authorities felt that *The Lower Depths* would be a total failure.

Rehearsals began immediately. According to Stanislavsky, the actors had difficulty putting across the feverish language of the play, "full of pretentious aphorisms and incoherent expressions in the tone of a sermon." "Those didactic, moralizing monologues must be recited simply," he said, "without letting the natural outflow of feeling be diverted by theatrical pathos. Otherwise there is danger of falling into melodrama."

To make themselves better able to convey the atmosphere of Moscow's "lower depths," the Art Theater company went to the Khitrov market, where beggars, thieves, and tramps lived. The actors visited foul-smelling dormitories where ragged men and women lay in disorder on wretched beds, they talked with the "intellectuals" of the place, and they were struck by the accuracy of the picture that Gorky had drawn in his play.

During rehearsals, Gorky especially appreciated the beauty and talent of a young red-haired actress, Maria Fedorovna Andreyeva, who came from a family of theater people. Her respectable position as a wife of a high official in the government railroad department had not prevented her from becoming an ardent supporter of far-left political doctrines. She kept subversive brochures hidden in her apartment, collected money for illegal organizations, and had finally even joined the Bolshevik Party. With fierce energy, she carried on both her artistic activities and her clandestine work. In the party, she had been nicknamed "The Phenomenon." Gorky had met her in 1900, in Sebastopol and Yalta, where she was on tour with the Art Theater. She had been immediately captivated by him when she saw him come into her dressing room with Chekhov. "Gorky seemed immense to me," she wrote in her memoirs. "It was only later that I realized he was slender, thin, that his back was bent and his chest hollow. He wore a Russian blouse, high boots, a broad-brimmed, strangely wrinkled hat that almost touched the ceiling, and a kind of cape over his shoulders in spite of the heat. He had kept his hat on when he came into my dressing room. . . . And suddenly his blue eyes shone between his long lashes, his lips formed a charming, childlike smile, his face seemed to me more beautiful than beauty, and my heart leapt for joy."

In Moscow, during rehearsals of *The Lower Depths*, their relations became more intimate. As the date of the opening performance drew closer, he felt his anxiety over his play growing, along with his admiration, affection, and respect for his favorite actress.

Contrary to the authorities' expectation, the play was triumphantly successful. The vitality of the text, the precision of the staging, and the realism of the acting aroused the enthusiasm of a public avid for strong emotions. The audience applauded, cheered, threw flowers, called for the author. Pushed onto the stage after the third act, Gorky appeared with a cigarette in his hand, overwhelmed, weeping tears of joy, not knowing how to thank that enraptured crowd. Carried away, Maria Andreyeva gave him her first kiss that evening.

After the performance, the whole troupe gathered in the Hermitage restaurant. Wearing his usual boots and black shirt, Gorky seemed out of place among the elegantly dressed actresses. Everyone in the room had eyes only for him. "Gorky became the hero of the day," wrote Stanislavsky. "He was followed in the street and at the theater; crowds of admirers—men, and especially women—clustered around him. At first he was sheepish about his popularity and behaved awkwardly, tugging at his short red mustache, constantly smoothing his long, stiff hair with his strong, manly fingers, or tossing back his head. He was so ill at ease that he would quiver, disconcerted, and bow. 'Listen, children,' he would say to his admirers with a guilty smile, 'this is really embarrassing. . . . It's true, I mean it! Why are you looking at me like that? I'm not a singer, or a ballerina. . . .' But his comical embarrassment, and his strange way of expressing himself in his agitation, only increased the number and interest of his partisans. His charm was powerful. He had his own kind off beauty and spontaneity, his own way of being."

His success was so great that the government newspapers were worried about it. *The Messenger* fulminated: "We must pity a society that, foolishly losing its self-awareness, forgetting its principles and traditions, and giving in to moral corruption, rushes to the spectacle of novelty like the mob in the time of the Caesars and wildly applauds the stench, filth, and vice of revolutionary propaganda . . . while the leader of the derelicts, Maxim Gorky, using his pen as a lever, shakes the ground on which that society was built. What a dangerous writer! How wretched and blind are his admirers, readers, and spectators!"

In an effort to limit the triumph of *The Lower Depths*, the government took the drastic step of requiring a special authorization for each performance and demanding the use of an expurgated text. The play was forbidden altogether in working-class theaters and in languages of the empire other than Russian. Despite this, however, it was acclaimed in many provincial towns and, in translation, extended its success into foreign countries. When it was published, its sales were unprecedented: the first edition of forty thousand copies was sold out in two weeks, and thirty-five thousand more were sold within less than a year.

Meanwhile, Gorky had become his own publisher by affiliating himself with a publishing firm called Knowledge, to which he attracted many "realistic" writers, including Leonid Andreyev and Ivan Bunin. Although he belonged to no political group, Andreyev was sympathetic to the revolution. He often made fun of the czar, that "little Nicholas" whose presence at the head of the country "marred the Russian landscape." Now and then he attended a clandestine meeting of students. The Okhrana kept an eye on him. Gorky admired him, but reproached him for being a solitary, cerebral, tormented writer who held himself aloof from the life of the masses and wallowed in morbid introspection. Their friendship was stormy. As for Bunin, an elegant yet powerful poet and short-story writer, he steadfastly refrained from all subversive activity, which irritated Gorky. They had in common only their negative attitude toward the decadent literary tendencies that were cultivated in the little coteries of St. Petersburg and Moscow. But Bunin criticized those "novelties" from a purely esthetic viewpoint, whereas Gorky condemned them as "Manifestations of the bourgeois mentality."

The bourgeois mentality had become his *bête noire*. He had an almost physical aversion to the propertied classes, even though they were partly responsible for his success. He expressed his literary credo in a letter to the writer Eleonsky on September 13, 1904: "For whom and for what do you write? You must think hard about that question. You must realize that in our time the best and most valuable readers, as well as the most attentive and demanding, are democratic workers and peasants who know how to read and write. What they look for in a book is, above all, answers to their social and moral concerns, to their basic impetus toward freedom, in the full meaning of the word. They vaguely sense many things. They sense that the falsity of our life is crushing them; they would like to understand that falsity and rid themselves of it."

The more Gorky's popularity grew in drawing rooms, universities, and factories, the more resentment it aroused in far-right circles. Toward the end of 1903 he was nearly killed by one of their henchmen. While he was walking along the Volga one evening, a man tried to stab him in the heart. The blade pierced his overcoat and jacket but, luckily, was stopped by a cigarette case. News of this attack shook public opinion and made Gorky even more highly valued by everyone who saw him as embodying the disaffection of the masses. Soon an important literary prize, the Griboyedov, was awarded to *The Lower Depths.* Gorky was already thinking about a new play: *Summer Folk.*

The climate in Russia, however, was not favorable to literature. Hostilities with Japan had just begun with the bombardment of Port Arthur, and the Japanese were invading Korea. Revolutionary passion was encouraged by the absurdity of that far-off war, its heavy casualties, and the incompetence of the Russian high command. People on the political right were worried about the future; those on the left hoped for a general cataclysm that would sweep away the czarist regime. Gorky, of course, condemned the war and called on the people to demonstrate in favor of ending it immediately.

In the midst of this agitation he learned that Chekhov had died on July 2, 1904, in the little German town of Badenweiler. Although he had been expecting that premature death, it threw him into consternation, like the death of a deeply loved parent. Chekhov's body was taken to Moscow. Gorky attended the funeral, with Chaliapin beside him, and angrily noted the frivolity and indifference of the crowd that had gathered to honor that strong, discreet writer. But the next day he was again caught up in the whirlwind of everyday life.

He was infuriated by the disastrous turn the war had taken at the front and the harsh demands of the government at home. This time he did not hesitate to preach violence against the police. At a public meeting he said, "If a demonstration takes place in the street on the twenty-eighth of November, don't let yourselves be whipped and trampled. Use pistols, knives, and even your teeth if necessary, to disorganize the police force that defends the present regime. Otherwise, street demonstrations will be meaningless."

In that same month of November 1904, the actress and producer Vera Komissarzhevskaya produced Gorky's third play, *Summer Folk*. In it, he again attacked the decadent bourgeois intellectuals who hid their moral weakness behind the hollow precepts of liberalism, and he contrasted them with the enlightened, energetic, and clear-headed proletariat, on whom the Russian future depended. This attitude toward the timorous liberals immediately won the approval of the Social Democrats, especially the hard-liners among them, who denounced "apolitical" writing. Although he was not a member of the party, Gorky became its most outstanding champion.

At the first performance of *Summer Folk*, the audience was turbulent. The end of the play was greeted by shouting and whistling. The uproar was directed from the box occupied by Merezhkovsky, Filosofov, and the staff of *The World of Art*. In the pit, indignant monarchists and liberals defied the extremists who acclaimed Gorky as a genius and shouted to him, "Thank-you, comrade! Hurrah! Down with the bourgeoisie!" Both sides felt that they had just witnessed not a play but a propaganda demonstration or a political rally. As for Gorky, he was elated at having set off that storm. Braving the tumult, he appeared downstage with the actors. "That première was the best day of my life . . ." he wrote to his wife on November 12. "I have never felt so deeply—and probably never will again . . . my own strength, my meaning in life, as I did at that moment when I stood before the footlights, not bowing my head to the audience, ready for all sorts of madness if anyone should take it into his head to boo me. . . . Near the footlights, people in the audience were frenziedly shouting incomprehensible words, with their cheeks glowing and their eyes blazing. Someone was sobbing and screaming insults, others were waving handkerchiefs, and I looked at them all, trying to find enemies and seeing only slaves and a few friends. . . . I felt as if I were a lion tamer."

The liberal press was stern, reprimanding Gorky for knowing nothing of the "torments of conscience" and the concern with "inner improvement" that all true intellectuals experienced. But he cared nothing about psychology, a bourgeois invention. He wanted to celebrate strong, primitive feelings. The hero of *Summer Folk*, the proletarian Vlass, contrasted with the ridiculous poetess Kaleria by his healthy brutality. The day after the dress rehearsal, a journalist wrote, "Today, on the stage, there is one Vlass shouting, but tomorrow, in life, thousands of Vlasses will begin shouting." That was what Gorky hoped.

11

BLOODY SUNDAY

In 1901, to oppose socialist propaganda, the government had the idea of creating workers' organizations controlled by agents of the Okhrana. One of those agents, the resourceful Father Georgi Gapon, founded a large association among factory workers in St. Petersburg and convinced them that all their troubles were caused by thickheaded employers, but that the czar, who loved them as his children, would listen sympathetically to their complaints. This movement, whose goal was to arouse love of the sovereign in the working masses, was successful beyond its leaders' expectations. Intoxicated by his popularity, Gapon decided to stage a gigantic peaceful demonstration on Sunday, January 9, 1905. A crowd of workers, accompanied by their wives and children and preceded by icons and religious banners, would go to the czar and present him with a petition requesting his protection and the election of a constituent assembly by universal suffrage.

Czar Nicholas II was at Tsarskoye Selo (now Pushkin).

Misguided by his close advisers, he refused to come to St. Petersburg to receive the "rioters." Detachments of soldiers were massed in the city to block the path of the procession. When he learned of this decision, Gorky went with a delegation of prominent political and literary figures to see Sergey Witte, the minister of the interior, to convince him that the procession of workers was harmless and that the troops concentrated around the Winter Palace should be withdrawn. Witte was unwilling to listen. The result was disaster. On the scheduled day, the unarmed crowd came up against the troops. The workers' ranks were broken by a Cossack charge, and then, when they were closing again, the soldiers began firing into them. Panic-stricken, the demonstrators ran away leaving hundreds of dead and wounded behind.

After seeing this senseless massacre, Gorky went home, overwhelmed with emotion. Many friends joined him. Fearing a house search, they burned the red flag they had brought back from the demonstration. "I remember how sadly Alexey Maximovich [Gorky] held it in his hands before burning it," Voitkevich, a witness to the scene, wrote in his memoirs. Gorky immediately wrote an appeal to public opinion that was to be signed by all members of the delegation. In it he said that Nicholas II had been informed that the demonstration would be peaceful. "Yet he authorized the slaughter of his innocent subjects by soldiers, and we therefore accuse him, personally, of murdering people who had done nothing to provoke such reprisals." He concluded: "We declare that such a regime can no longer be tolerated and we call on all citizens of Russia to begin struggling immediately, tenaciously, and fraternally against autocracy." That evening he announced at a public meeting that, for him, the revolution had begun. And he wrote to his wife, Ekaterina, who had remained in Nizhni Novgorod, "So the Russian revolution has begun. . . . The dead do not disturb me; history takes on a new color only through blood."

He gave the text of his appeal to the members of the delegation so that it would be published with the greatest possible number of signatures. But on the night of January 11, 1905, the police seized the manuscript from one of the members and recognized its author's handwriting. Gorky, who had hurriedly left St. Petersburg, was arrested in Riga, taken back to the capital, and imprisoned in the dreaded Peter and Paul Fortress. His home was searched, but without result. Even so, he was absurdly accused of having tried to set up a "provisional government" to rule Russia after the revolution. Taking advantage of his isolation in a cell, he wrote his fourth play, *The Children of the Sun*, which he himself judged to be a failure. At this time, with all the tragic events that were occurring in his country, it was hard for him to be detached from them and devote himself to a work of imagination.

His arrest had set off a wave of protest in Russia. There were spontaneous demonstrations in streets, theaters, and universities. Even foreigners were disturbed by the feudal repression of a writer whose only crime was publicly expressing his ideas. Newspapers all over the world published indignant articles demanding Gorky's release. An avalanche of petitions from France, Germany, Austria, and Italy, signed by eminent people in those countries, fell onto the desks of Russian government ministers. In Paris, the Society of Friends of the Russian People and the Annexed Peoples, headed by Anatole France, published this appeal: "To all free men. The great writer Maxim Gorky is about to appear before a special court, charged with plotting against the security of the state. His crime is having tried to place himself, when there was still time, between loaded rifles and the chests of defenseless workers. The czar's government wants to punish him for that crime. . . . It is impossible that the world's conscience will placidly allow that legal outrage to be committed. . . . All men worthy of the name must defend those sacred rights in the person of Gorky."

The czar's government was troubled by this unanimous disapproval. The authorities had not expected such an uproar over the routine arrest of a protesting writer. Moreover, the Okhrana officials assigned to investigate the new "Peshkov affair" found it hard to establish the defendant's guilt in accordance with the penal code: Gorky's membership in the delegation was not a criminal act, since the delegation's goal was to forestall street disturbances by calling the attention of the authorities to the danger of a confrontation between the army and the demonstrators.

After a month in prison, Gorky was provisionally released on ten thousand rubles' bail, with orders to stay in St. Petersburg and cooperate with the preliminary investigation of his case. But the chief of police had no desire to leave such a troublesome man in the capital. He had Gorky sent to Riga, accompanied by an Okhrana agent. In the hotel where he stayed, two spies were assigned to watch him. Although he was glad to be out of prison, he felt that he was in an equivocal position. Maybe his enemies would accuse him of avoiding a trial out of cowardice. To cut short any malicious interpretation of his departure, he wrote to the publisher Piatnitsky on February 27, "Trying to avoid a trial is out of the question for me. On the contrary, it is indispensable for me to be tried. If they decide to end this stupid affair by administrative action, I will make it burst out again, more fully and in a brighter light, and I will obtain justice for myself and dishonor for the Romanovs and those who follow them. If the trial takes place and I am convicted, that will give me an excellent opportunity to explain to Europe why I am a 'revolutionary' and what reasons I have for my 'crimes against the established order,' an order that manifests itself in the slaughter of peaceful, unarmed Russian citizens, including children."

A few days later, on March 5, he wrote an open letter to Tolstoy, reproaching him for being preoccupied with the moral improvement of individuals in that time of social upheaval: "Consider, Leo Nikolayevich, whether one can think of one's moral improvement when the state is shooting men and women in city streets and then preventing help from being given to the wounded."

The government was still undecided about the attitude it ought to take toward Gorky. Should it open a public trial and risk a new explosion of indignation all over the world? Should there be a closed trial? Should the whole affair be hushed up? Because of recent political events, the authorities were strongly inclined to be cautious. Successive defeats in the war against Japan were matched by strikes and mass demonstrations at home.

In June 1905, the crew of the battleship *Potemkin*, of the Black Sea fleet, mutinied in protest against the bad quality of their food; they killed several officers, hoisted the red flag, took the ship to Odessa to support a workers' insurrection there, and, when the insurrection failed, continued on to a Rumanian port, where the mutineers were disarmed and interned. This mutiny, unprecedented in the imperial navy, encouraged the revolutionaries to intensify their propaganda in the armed forces.

In the autumn of 1905, the hard-pressed czar finally agreed to make some concessions: he granted the constitution that the liberals had been demanding, and the legal proceedings against Gorky were dropped. Moving back and forth between St. Petersburg and Moscow, Gorky took part in public meetings, wrote proclamations, and made strenuous efforts to convince the workers and intellectuals that the government's recent backing down should incite them to make still more demands. On October 17, Nicholas II issued a manifesto in which he promised to convene a legislative assembly, the Duma.

Meanwhile, Gorky and his Social Democrat friends had founded a large daily, *New Life*, the first legal Bolshevik newspaper. Its inaugural issue appeared on October 27. Part of the money needed for it had come from Gorky himself: thanks to his royalties, he now had a very comfortable income. His days of heroic poverty were over. He now rebelled without lacking anything, on principle, thinking of others. But his positions were so radical that he was afraid he might have to confront the reactionary gangs known as the Black Hundreds. He therefore agreed to have eight husky, resolute Georgian Bolsheviks stay with him to defend him against any attacks that might occur. The Black Hundreds had recently killed a revolutionary named Bauman, whose funeral, on October 20, had given rise to immense demonstrations with shouts of "Down with despotism!"

It was in *New Life* that Gorky published his famous *Notes on the Petty Bourgeois Mentality*. "I know of no more vicious enemies of life than the petty bourgeoisie," he wrote. "They want to reconcile the oppressor and the martyr. They teach the martyr patience and persuade him not to oppose the violence done to him; they try to demonstrate the impossibility of changing relations between the haves and the have-nots; they promise the people a reward in heaven for their toil and suffering, and, while admiring their hard life on earth, suck their vital forces like lice. Most of them are directly in the service of constraint; the rest contribute to it indirectly and preach acceptance, conciliation, forgiveness, acquittal." Carried away by his passion, he denounced bourgeois tendencies in the works of Dostoyevsky and Tolstoy.

It was on November 27, 1905, that he first met Lenin, who had just returned from exile firmly determined to speed up the process of the regime's disintegration. "We saw each other in St. Petersburg, I don't remember exactly where," Gorky later said. "He was short, with an ironic look in his eyes. I was tall and badly built, with the face and bearing of a Mordvin.[1] At first, things didn't go well between us. Then we looked at each other a little more attentively and conversation suddenly became easier." Though Lenin admired Gorky and approved of his brutal attacks against the bourgeoisie, he deplored his sentimental attachment to certain liberals. Gorky wanted the editorial staff of *New Life* to include both zealous Bolsheviks and nonmilitant leftist writers, so that the paper would be truly democratic, whereas Lenin demanded the expulsion of everyone who did not belong to the party, in order to create a close-knit team blindly devoted to Marxist ideas. *New Life* took on such an aggressive tone that, on December 2, it was shut down by the government. Its place in the struggle was taken over by other publications, some of them on the fringes of legality.

On December 7, a general strike, instigated by the Bolsheviks, paralyzed Moscow. Gorky helped distribute weapons to the strikers. His apartment had become an operational center for organizing street fighting. The first clashes with government forces were violent and bloody. Hastily erected barricades resisted all assaults. "A wonderful battle!" Gorky wrote to Piatnitsky on December 10. "Cannons are thundering. It began yesterday afternoon at three o'clock, it went on all night, and today there is still constant firing. The workers are behaving admirably. . . . Near the Nikolai station, corpses are strewn over the pavement. Five cannons and two machine guns are in action there, but the workers, fraternally united, make every effort to fight back against the troops. . . . The fighting has spread all over Moscow."

Political meetings were already being held in several regiments, and some soldiers no longer hid their sympathy with the rebels. Since the Moscow garrison was not reliable, on December 16, the government sent in the Semionovsky regiment, with artillery, from St. Petersburg. Three days later the insurrection had been crushed, and thousands had been killed or wounded. After that bloodbath, Moscow became calm again. The country began breathing more easily, though without knowing whether it had escaped a great danger or missed a chance for political renewal. After all, things seemed to be working out well: Russia had a Duma, freedom of assembly and freedom of the press were practically assured, and the Treaty of Portsmouth had put an end to the humiliating war with Japan. Yet a proclamation by Gorky was being circulated clandestinely: "The proletariat is not defeated, even though it has suffered losses. The revolution has been strengthened by hope, its leadership has been considerably expanded. . . . The Russian proletariat is on its way to a decisive victory because it is the only class in the country that is morally sound, clear-headed, and sure of its future."

Gorky had never before felt so "necessary." But in that reactionary climate his personal situation was becoming more and more precarious. He was likely to be arrested again. To remove him from that danger, his Bolshevik friends suggested that he go to the United States. There he could take advantage of his international fame to collect money for the party's treasury. That would still be a way of serving the cause. Gorky immediately accepted the suggestion and began preparing for his departure in great secrecy.

12

THE EXILE'S RAGE

In deciding to go abroad, Gorky realized that he was acting not only in his comrades' interest, but also in accordance with his own personal preference. While he no longer had any doubts about the need to struggle against despotism, for some time he had been feeling uneasy in his private life. In 1903, after seven years of marriage, he had separated from his wife Ekaterina Peshkov. But they had not officially divorced and there was no total break between them. Though they lived apart, they still had bonds of affection, trust, and esteem. The children, Max and Katiusha, lived with their mother.

For the time being, Gorky had united his life with Maria Andreyeva's. Passionately devoted to him, she gave up the theater to go with him in all his travels and adventures. But although he was genuinely in love with her, he never showed his feelings for her in public. In his letters he wrote profusely about his political passions, but he never said a word to his friends about his love life. It was as if he wanted to remain in shadow so that light could be concentrated on his activities in the revolutionary struggle.

When Gorky asked Maria Andreyeva to go abroad with him in the line of duty and work toward the revolution from outside Russia, she eagerly consented. Aside from everything else, she would be useful to him as an interpreter, since she spoke several foreign languages and he spoke none.

They secretly left together, went first to Finland, and reached Berlin in February 1906. Europe had long since discovered Gorky. His works were published by six German companies; in France, an enthusiastic study by Melchior de Vogüé had increased his fame still more; *The Lower Depths* and *The Children of the Sun* were performed in Berlin theaters with great success; his books, and pictures of him, were prominently displayed in bookstore windows. Soon after his arrival, Max Reinhardt, who reigned over the German theater, organized a benefit performance for him. When Gorky appeared on the stage, the audience stood up to greet him with admiring shouts of *"Hoch!"* The money taken in that evening was given to the Bolshevik Party.

After meeting August Bebel, leader of the German Social Democrats, Gorky felt that he had nothing more to do in Germany and went to Paris, where a crucial task awaited him. In that spring of 1906, the Russian government, financially ruined by the stupid Russo-Japanese war, was negotiating with the Western nations for a loan that would enable it to put its internal situation back in order. Gorky's mission was to arouse French public opinion against this kind of help to the czarist regime. On April 9, the newspaper *L'Humanité* (edited at that time by Jean Jaurès) published an article by him with the title "Not One Sou to the Russian Government."

This article was vigorously approved by the Society of Friends of the Russian People, whose members, besides Anatole France, included Steinlen, Mirbeau, Langlois, and Seignebos. Gorky immediately wrote to Anatole France to express his gratitude: "My deeply respected comrade in arms, the day when I learned that a Society of Friends of the Russian People had been formed in France was a day of great joy for me. . . . Your feelings toward the Russian people not only confirm my faith in the power of art but also revive the idea of the brotherhood of peoples. . . . My country is the scene of senseless, vicious, unspeakable violence against humanity. . . . Having been crushed by the Romanovs and their rapacious desire to strengthen an authority that they themselves have made invalid through their incompetence and cruelty, my people are now beginning to hold up their heads again. . . . All upright, brave, and sincere men and women have sided with the people; everyone realizes that only the people's energy can save the country from ruin, and even the priests, their former enemies, now march at the head of the rebellious peasants. The degenerate, incompetent Romanovs, wanting to continue dominating the country at any cost and panic-stricken at the thought of losing their power, have surrounded themselves with the most contemptible, ferocious, and infamous creatures in Russia. . . . The struggle will be neither long nor difficult if Europe does not give the Russian government money to perpetrate massacres and executions. . . . But if the state of tension in which the people are living is prolonged still more, they will store up reserves of cruelty and hatred in their souls, and at the decisive moment, which cannot be avoided, the outpouring of that cruelty will terrify the world. . . . Sincere friends of humanity must help the Russian people to throw off the yoke of those who pervert their souls, their gentle, deep and beautiful souls."

The Society of Friends of the Russian People published this letter in the form of a brochure, with a reply by Anatole France: "Maxim Gorky, I salute and honor you because you, a poet and man of action, have had the privilege of suffering for the cause served by your genius. That cause will triumph; desire and love create life. . . . I send you, the president of the Society of Friends of the Russian People, my wishes for the success of the liberating revolution, and I confide to you the indignation I feel at the thought that French financiers might provide money to the government of hangmen that tortures a magnanimous people."

Despite this show of opposition, the French banks, encouraged by the government, agreed to grant the loan. And Gorky indignantly responded with a vehement pamphlet. Addressing himself to "Fair France," he wrote, "Your best children no longer know you . . . a woman kept by bankers. . . . You, the Mother of Liberty, you, Joan of Arc, have allowed beasts to try to crush men once again. O great France, once the guide of civilization, do you realize the vileness of your act? Your money-grubbing hand has tried to stop a whole country from taking the road to freedom and culture. . . . O my beloved, I spit blood and gall into your eyes."

This coarse diatribe offended most of the French journalists who had championed Gorky's cause when he was imprisoned in the Peter and Paul Fortress. They did not understand how this man, whose release they had demanded, could thank them by insulting their country. Having belatedly learned of their acrimonious attacks on him, Gorky replied to them with two letters published in *L'Humanité* on December 11, 1906, under the title "To My Detractors."

The first letter, relatively moderate in tone, was addressed to the historian Aulard: "I spoke [in my article] about the France of bankers and financiers, of policemen and ministers: I spat in the face of that France, which jeered at Emile Zola. . . . The Russian revolution will develop slowly and for a long time, but it will end with the victory of the people . . ." And he concluded with this prophetic statement: "I am sure that the Russian people will not reimburse the bankers of France for those loans, which they have already repaid with their blood. No, they will not!" The second letter, harsh and contemptuous, was addressed to Alfred-Léon Gérault-Richard, René Viviani, and Jules Claretie: "'I was nice to you, so you ought to repay me with your gratitude,' that is what I gather from your words. But, gentlemen, I feel no gratitude to you for your generosity; I believe it is only a misunderstanding. . . . When you protest against it [my imprisonment], your conduct—allow me to speak this truth—makes me laugh. For we are enemies, and irreconcilable enemies, I am sure. The honest writer is always an enemy of our present society, and with even greater reason he is an enemy of those who defend and justify the greed and lust for domination that are the foundation of today's social organization. . . . Gentlemen, I tell you very sincerely that to me, a socialist, your bourgeois love is deeply offensive."

Gorky still had not given up his intention of going to the United States. In April 1906, he and Maria Andreyeva left Cherbourg on a ship bound for New York. The American public knew he was coming. The Russian ambassador in Washington had suggested that the American government keep out this troublemaker by applying a law that forbade anarchists to enter the country, but it was decided that the law did not apply to Gorky. Questioned by an immigration official who came aboard the ship at New York, Gorky answered proudly, "No, I am not an anarchist. I am a socialist. I respect law and order. That, in fact, is why I am opposed to the Russian government, which now represents organized anarchy."

When he left the ship, he was cheered by a crowd that had gathered on the dock and included many émigrés. Reporters came to interview him in his hotel at the corner of Broadway and 77th Street. Maria served as his interpreter. Then, despite his fatigue, he had to attend a banquet given in his honor by a writers' club. Among the guests was Mark Twain, in person. In his reply to the welcoming speeches, Gorky said, "Now the time to abolish czarism has finally come!"

But the Russian government counterattacked: its ambassador informed the American press that the woman traveling with Gorky was not his wife. In the climate of exacerbated puritanism then reigning in the United States, this revelation had the effect of a bomb. The *World*, a reactionary New York newspaper, led the fight in the name of morality. After being the heroes of the day, Gorky and Maria were suddenly shunned as if they had the plague. One evening when they were about to go up to their room, they were met by the hotel manager, who, with her face contorted by anger, ordered them to leave immediately. Their suitcases had already been brought down to the lobby. No other hotel was willing to take them. As a last resort, they took refuge in the writers' club where they had dined on the evening of their arrival. But they were asked not to show themselves at the windows.

A little later, several Americans braved the scandal and wrote to the two undesirables to offer temporary hospitality. Gorky accepted the offer of a couple, Mr. and Mrs. Martin, who lived in a house on Staten Island. There he found an atmosphere of friendship and tolerance that contrasted with the animosity of most of the public. A few freethinkers appreciated the speeches he gave at various political meetings, but most intellectuals, influenced by newspaper articles on his private life, virtuously kept their distance from him. Mark Twain refused to preside over another banquet in Gorky's honor. The few leftist Americans were reluctant to answer appeals for contributions to the Bolshevik Party. Instead of the expected millions, the money collected only came to about ten thousand dollars.

New York amazed and revolted Gorky. Lost in that gigantic, noisy, teeming city, with its haughtily tall buildings, its smoke, its luxury shops, and its slums full of humiliated black people, the son of the Volga felt hatred of insolent Yankee prosperity growing steadily inside him. Having come to solicit money for a noble cause, he now found that he had the soul of a biblical prophet fulminating against his contemporaries' wicked ways. The lightning of socialist morality flashed in his fist. He was glad to leave New York to spend the summer in the country house that the Martins owned in the Adirondacks, near the Canadian border.

It was there that he received a telegram from Ekaterina

telling him that their daughter, Katiusha, had died, probably
of tuberculosis. Grief-stricken, he answered on August 20,
1906, "It's very sad. I pity my little girl, but I pity you even
more. I know you're hurt, wounded, and I can see your bewil-
dered, frightened face. . . . Lately I've been expecting and
waiting for something tragic, and now it's happened."

He worried about his son, Max. Was he, too, predisposed
to tuberculosis? Gorky's stay in the United States seemed
more and more painful to him. "If you only knew, if you could
only see how I live here," he wrote to Ekaterina in late August
or early September. "I'm the most horrible man in this country. A newspaper has written, 'The nation has never known
such humiliation and degradation as those inflicted on it by
that mad Russian anarchist who has no sense of morality and
amazes everyone by his hatred of religion, order, and even
people.' Another one reports a speech given in the Senate,
asking to have me deported. . . . Hostile signs are put on the
door of the house where I'm living."

Despite that campaign of harassment, Gorky refused to let
himself become disheartened. He was now hard at work on a
proletarian novel, *Mother*, and a play, *Enemies*. In writing
Mother, he was inspired by events that had taken place at the
Sormovo factories in 1902, and his heroes—the worker Pavel
Vlassov and the illiterate peasant woman Nilovna—were
modeled on real people he had known in Nizhni Novgorod.
The story shows simple, primitive minds coming to realize the
beauty of the socialist promise. Vlassov gradually frees himself from his servile habits, discovers the light of intellect,
and enters into the revolutionary struggle. His mother, Nilovna, seeing how workers have been subjected to injustice
for endless years, volunteers to hand out leaflets, without car-
ing about the danger. These workers do not selfishly limit
their concern to improving their own lot: they demand a radical change in human relations; they want to alter the face of
the world.

The novel appeared in an American magazine in 1906,

then in book form in New York and London, but the un-
abridged Russian text was published only in Berlin. In Russia
only the first part, savagely censured, was published in 1907,
and it was quickly taken off the market by the police. A
government press committee even decided to prosecute Gorky
for "propagating a work that advocates serious violations of
the law, provokes the hostility of workers against the proper-
ties classes, and calls for riots and acts of rebellion." This
stern measure did not prevent distribution of the Berlin Rus-
sian-language edition; thousands of copies of it were smuggled into the country. Furthermore, the leftist press in
Germany, France, and Italy published translations of the
novel, either in serial form or as a newspaper supplement.
Ultimately, the prohibition of *Mother* only increased its success.

The play *Enemies*, animated by the same spirit of class
struggle, was also prohibited in Russia. But it seemed that
each blow struck against Gorky made him still more famous.
A whole world of money acclaimed him and knelt before him
while he detested it and looked down on it from the height of
his growing renown. During his stay in the United States he
wrote a series of angry political tirades against his American
hosts: "The City of the Yellow Devil," "In America," "My
Interviews."

In "My Interviews," in the course of imaginary conversations with the great of this world, he stigmatized American
capitalism, German militarism, and the greed of French financiers. Elsewhere, he denounced the horror of bourgeois
democracy, which, behind a false front of morality, based its
prosperity on the poverty of the people. To him, New York
symbolized the subjection of the human race to the Almighty
Dollar: "It seems that an enormous block of gold whirls at the
center of the city with terrible speed and a voluptuous hiss.
All day long it scatters little particles of itself in the streets,
and all day long people seek, catch, and eagerly grab
them. . . . To do this, from morning to night they dig in the

earth, forge iron, build houses, inhale the smoke of factories, breathe sick, poisoned air. . . . This evil spell numbs their souls and turns them into docile instruments of the yellow devil." And in another passage: "I have seen much poverty, I am well acquainted with its greenish, bloodless, bony face. . . . But the horror of poverty on the [Lower] East Side goes beyond anything I have seen elsewhere." So in the United States, proud of its wealth, order, and industrial power, Gorky saw only falsehood, frivolity, and exploitation of the weak by the strong, of the poor by the rich. And, in his opinion, Europe was no better.

Where could he go to escape the curse of imperialism and capitalism? After his attacks against the "Judas loan" solicited by the czar, going back to Russia was out of the question for him, and he had treated the Western nations so harshly in his pamphlets that they also considered him undesirable. The émigré Russian writer Filosofov sharply took him to task in the April 1907 issue of *The Russian Word*, a magazine published in Paris: "Perhaps Europe really is horrible, and perhaps it seems especially so to a Russian, but Gorky has condemned it in such a tone, and has shown such misunderstanding of the real European mind, and, above all, has given his aggression such an inartistic form, that anyone with any impartiality at all feels an irresistible desire to come to Europe's defense. . . . With the thoughtlessness of a barbarian, he has hurled defiance at all of France: 'I spit blood and gall into your eyes.' But France did not flinch and we are ashamed for Gorky. . . . A man for whom no problem exists, and who has extinguished the fire of his soul with the dirty water of materialism, can only transform himself into an average self-satisfied bourgeois."

Since Italy was almost the only country that Gorky had not railed against, it was there that he decided to seek refuge. Before leaving, he said to a meeting of American workers, "I am going to the other side of the ocean, because there I will be closer to the revolution, and I will be able to continue working for freedom." On September 30, 1907,[1] he and Maria left New York for Naples.

The Italians greeted him as a conquering hero. A joyous crowd, restrained by the police only with difficulty, gathered in front of his hotel and shouted, "Long live Gorky! Long live the great writer! Long live the Russian revolution!" In a lecture on October 15 (October 28), he said to his electrified audience, "When someone speaks of my revolutionary activity I feel moved and ashamed, because I am only an ordinary soldier in the great army of the Russian revolution. Accepting your welcome as a tribute to revolutionary Russia, I thank you for myself, for my country, and in the name of the international proletariat."

Five days later he took a boat to Capri. Though he went to that island with the intention of staying only a short time, he would spend seven years there.

13

CAPRI

Situated in the lower part of the island of Capri, the house where Gorky stayed was large, opulently furnished, and surrounded by a flowery garden, with a magnificent view of the sea. At first this bourgeois luxury made him a little uncomfortable, as if he had put on someone else's clothes. But Maria, who watched over his health and his good spirits, soon convinced him that he needed that calm in order to continue his work.

He contemplated the island's scenery and had no contact with its inhabitants. Never for one moment did he consider learning Italian, or any other foreign language. Transplanted, he disdained the blue water of the Gulf of Naples, the beds of roses, the orderly vineyards, the azure grottoes, and Vesuvius smoking in the distance, and he dreamed only of the banks of the Volga, the bare steppes, and the twilight wind in birch forests. To him the real world was not the world he had before his eyes, but the one he had left behind when he fled from his country. His homesickness was so great that he wrote, "If a tooth pulled out of a jaw could feel anything, it would probably feel as lonely as I do." It was in Capri that he conceived one of his most characteristic stories: "The Little Town of Okurov," a gloomy picture of the mean-spirited, stagnant life of the petty bourgeoisie in an out-of-the-way corner of the Russian provinces.

Now and then he left his island and went to Naples, Florence, Rome, or Genoa, but he always came back to his home port. Increasingly, numerous visitors came to Capri to pay their respects to the master in his "gilded cage"; some were writers or artists, some were simply sightseers, and most were Marxists. Like Tolstoy at Yasnaya Polyana, Gorky on his island was surrounded by a court in which beggars mingled with admirers, idle travelers with truth-seekers. He received and listened to everyone carefully and eagerly: those echoes from his native land were necessary to his survival under a foreign sky. Letters from Russia piled up on his desk—letters from writers, scholars, political sympathizers, ordinary workers. Although they were often incorrectly addressed, Gorky was so well known in Italy that they always reached him. Buried under manuscripts, confessions, requests for advice, and pleas for money, he made it a rule to read them all attentively and to answer them, point by point, as soon as possible. Remembering his own difficult beginnings, he could not bear, out of laziness or neglect, to ignore appeals from humble people. His table was open to everyone, and noisy. Some guests prolonged their stay for weeks.

Maria Andreyeva was with him, acting not only as mistress of the house but also as his nurse and secretary. She typed his manuscripts; filed his correspondence; translated articles in French, English, German and Italian newspapers for him; and served as his interpreter when he had foreign visitors. His royalties, which he received regularly in Capri, made it possible for him to get along, but his liberality to the party and his help to compatriots in need were a strain on the family budget. When Maria was advised to reduce their expenditures by receiving fewer guests, for example, she replied, "No, no, that's impossible. Alexey Maximovich would notice it. He had to tear himself away from his country but, thanks to the comrades who come here to visit him, he still sees Russians. That's as necessary to him as breathing. I've taken over all money worries for him, and I can manage them. I'll see to it that he never has to write for money. His work has to be free of all financial concerns."

Although he was not a member of the Social Democratic Party, in 1907 Gorky was invited as a "guest of honor" to the party's congress in London. He was glad to go, because the delights of Capri were beginning to pall on him, but when he found himself in the midst of the three hundred militants who had gathered in London, he soon realized that some of them, like Axelrod and Deutsch, were more reformists than revolutionaries; and that others, like Plekhanov, were too European, not Russian enough, to be entitled to lead the workers' movement. Lenin, however, captivated him by his firmness and simplicity. "That bald . . . well-built man rubbed his forehead with one hand, like Socrates," he wrote in his *Reminiscences.* "Looking at me with his amazingly bright and lively eyes, he began telling me about the faults of my book *Mother.* He had borrowed the manuscript from my Berlin publisher, and quickly read it. I told him I had been in a hurry to write that book, without knowing exactly why. Lenin nodded and said, 'You were right to hurry, because it's a useful book. Many workers have taken part in the revolutionary movement without realizing it, spontaneously. Now they'll benefit from reading *Mother.* It's a book that's come out at the right time.' That was his only compliment, but it meant a great deal to me." Gorky was to keep that concept of the moral and social usefulness of literature for the rest of his life.

With Lenin and Maria, he went sightseeing in London, visited museums, and met famous writers, like George Bernard Shaw, H. G. Wells, and Thomas Hardy. "The congress [in London] was fascinating to me," he later wrote to Ekaterina. "The three weeks went by before I knew it, and I was enriched with healthy, vigorous impressions. I love workers, especially our own workers, the Bolsheviks. They are an extraordinarily lively, varied, and intelligent people, with such an open-minded interest in life! I organized a public meeting in Hyde Park; I talked about recent literature there, and I was surprised by the quality and intensity of my listeners' attention."

After the London congress, he went back to his "gilded cage" in Capri with a heightened feeling of solitude. He had a physical need for contact with the people. He was therefore enthusiastic when two great Bolshevik leaders, Lunacharsky and Bogdanov, asked him to create a school for propagandists in Capri. Without hesitation, he offered to let classes be held in his house. The list of lectures was long and resolutely Marxist. Gorky made himself the teacher of history and literature. The students were to be secretly recruited at working-class centers in Russia, and would cross the border with false papers to come to Italy and learn methods of clandestine struggle. As for the teachers, the organizing committee wanted them to be chosen from all the various factions of the party, so that all tendencies would be represented. But finally only Bolshevik theoreticians answered the invitation. So when the school took in its first group of students (about twenty), it was limited to militant Bolshevism rather than being an expression of Marxism in its entirety. And even among the Bolsheviks a serious division was about to take place. Lunacharsky, Bogdanov, and a few other eminent Marxists were trying to complete and "spiritualize" Marxism. They felt that in order for socialism to be fulfilled, it had to become a religion. This transition from an economic concept to an ideological and almost mystical concept was in accordance with Gorky's unavowed aspirations. His love for the people was visceral. He needed to believe in them, as the faithful believed in God.

Meanwhile, still guided by his devotion to the working masses, he had refused to take part in organizing a celebration of Tolstoy's eightieth birthday. "Count Leo Tolstoy is an artistic genius, perhaps our Shakespeare," he wrote to Vengerov in July 1908. "But for more than twenty years the chiming I have heard from that steeple has offended my convictions; for thirty years that old man has been constantly talking about transforming young, marvelous Russia into a Chinese province, and the new, talented Russian man into a slave. . . . Perhaps you find my judgment too harsh, and it may well be. But I cannot help it. I have paid more than enough for the right to think as I do."

In 1908, he published "The Confession," a story dedicated to Chaliapin in which he analyzed the moral conflict of a character drawn to both Marxism and Christianity. Matvei, the hero of the story, a foundling brought up by a deacon to respect the Holy Scriptures, wonders even in childhood why God has so little love for the people. When he grows up, he begins wandering in search of absolute truth. At the edge of a forest he meets an old pilgrim who gives him the solution to the problem: God still remains to be created, and it is factory workers who are carrying out that exemplary task. Matvei therefore goes to them and, enlightened by their wisdom, catches sight of the way that leads to a new God, a God of justice and kindness. But the police soon come after them and Matvei leaves the factory to preach the good word elsewhere. His faith is confirmed by a miracle: before the gates of a convent a pious, impassioned crowd surrounds a paralyzed young woman lying on a stretcher. Suddenly, as though galvanized by the power emanating from the people, who have invented God and carry him within them, she stands up and walks.

This mixture of mystical and social elements inevitably displeased Lenin, whose rigorous atheism allowed no departures from strict doctrine. He condemned "The Confession," and more generally the prophecies of Bogdanov and Lunacharsky, as attempts to deviate from the philosophy of Marx. He refused to come and teach a course in the new school, established a school of his own at Longjumeau, near Paris, and attracted a few students to it from the one in Capri. The directing committee of the Capri school reproached Lenin for his "disloyalty," and he accused his adversaries of wanting to create a new, non-Marxist party. He left Gorky out of the quarrel, however, as though his talent as a writer excused his political aberrations. He even went back to Capri in 1910 (after having spent two weeks there in 1908), at Gorky's invitation, and that meeting sealed their reconciliation.

The friendship between the two men was strangely based on the opposition of their natures. They appeared to be as antagonistic as ice and fire. Lenin, whose real name was Ulyanov, was the son of a school official and had practiced law. In all his decisions he was guided by inflexible logic. Clear-headed and cold, enclosed in a rigid system, he was always against making even the slightest concessions in ideology; he professed an unalloyed materialism; and he felt that where the revolution was concerned, the end justified the means. Gorky, a son of the people, with his artistic, emotional temperament, was capable of unthinking enthusiasm, sudden hatred and uncontrolled compassion. He had educated himself with his broad, somewhat random reading, and he had the self-taught man's respect for knowledge. From his childhood he still had a primitive religiosity that affected his revolutionary behavior. His socialism was not reasoned but intuitive, like the call of faith in an early Christian.

He had conceived great hopes for the future of the school in Capri, but after endless discussions it was closed down, and the students and teachers left the island.

Left alone with Maria, he sank into moodiness. The news from Russia was alarming. The failure of the 1905 revolution had been followed by a savage repression carried out by the minister of the interior, Pyotr Stolypin. The liberal intellectuals were disheartened. The proletariat was muzzled and no longer dared to hold up its head. In other countries, socialists of all varieties were clashing in sterile polemics, while in Russia autocracy was consolidating itself behind a false appearance of parliamentary government. Was Russia still capable of a burst of liberating energy? Another piece of news affected Gorky deeply: Tolstoy had died on November 7, 1910, in the little town of Astapovo, where he had gone to get away from his family.

At first, Gorky was appalled by that "escape"; he saw it as a pitiful bit of play-acting intended to serve Tolstoy's legend. "Leo Nikolayevich's [Tolstoy's] flight from his house and his family made me feel skeptical and almost angry with him," he wrote to Ekaterina, "because I know his old need to suffer, to put himself in agreement with his religious ideas and his preaching. I sensed something deliberate and premeditated in his flight. You know how much I hate that kind of sermon recommending a passive attitude toward life, and you must realize how harmful those Buddhist ideas are in a nation deeply impregnated with fatalism. . . . And suddenly a telegram from Rome announcing Leo Nikolayevich's death. . . . For five minutes I felt very strange. Then I sobbed. I locked myself in my room and wept desperately all day. I have never felt so much an orphan as I did that day; I have never felt such sadness over a man's death. . . . The most beautiful, most powerful and greatest man has left our life. . . . It is not only his wife who has been widowed, it is also Russian literature. . . . It is a judge who has left. I even miss the prophet intensely, yet I disliked him!"

The following year, Stolypin was assassinated at the opera house in Kiev, before the eyes of the czar and the czarina. But that act by an isolated revolutionary only served to strengthen political constraint. When he thought of his bound and stifled homeland, Gorky was ashamed of his Italian comfort. "I'm not in agreement with anything or anyone," he wrote to Ekaterina on January 12, 1912. "I quarrel with everyone, everything seems to me suspicious and false, and at the same time every-

thing makes me feel sorry for people: they are incredibly unhappy." And on January 30, "My life is very painful, more
and more painful. It seems to me that I am losing what was
most important and precious to me, what I was living for: my
faith in Russia and her future."

He now waited for visits from Russian travelers with the
impatience of an addict waiting for a dose of his drug. Each
newcomer was taken from the ship to shore in a boat. In the
little port, quarrelsome children surrounded him, took his
suitcase, and when they learned that he was going to see
Gorky, led him to the cable railway, shouting, *"Signore Gorky!
Molto ricco! Molto ricco!"* ("Mr. Gorky! Very rich! Very rich!")

Gorky's house was a former monastery transformed into a
middle-class home. In his study was a long table covered with
green cloth, high enough to let him write without bending
down. The immense window—a whole glazed wall—overlooked rocks and the blue sea. In the distance was Vesuvius,
with its plume of smoke. A terrace with a colonnade. A garden overflowing with flowers and exotic plants. And, in the
midst of that harmonious calm, a caged bear. All guests were
struck by the contrast between the elegance of the setting and
the gruffness of the man who had chosen to live in it.

Everyone gathered at the table for meals. Besides the usual
guests, there was now Zinovy Peshkov, Gorky's "adopted
son," a young man of twenty-eight whose real name was
Sverdlov.[1] Gorky had first taken an interest in him in about
1900, and had served as his godfather when at eighteen he
was baptized into the Russian Orthodox religion, a formality
he had to fulfill in order to be admitted into the Philharmonic
School. On that occasion, Gorky authorized him to use the
name of Peshkov. Although there was no official adoption,
emotional bonds between the "godfather" and the "godson"
were very close. In 1904, refusing to do his military service,
Zinovy Peshkov had gone to Canada, where he worked in a
fur-coat factory in Toronto. Then, after long wanderings in the
United States and New Zealand, he had come back to Russia,

and from there he had gone on to Capri. "My prodigal son
Zinovy has just arrived," Gorky wrote to Max on May 24,
1907. "He has been telling us very interesting things about
New Zealand and all sorts of savages." The adventurous
young man's stories amused Gorky and reminded him of his
own vagabond youth.

One of his guests, the Bolshevik militant Tatiana Alexinsky, wrote in her memoirs, "After a few hours of rest I sat
down in a spacious dining room flooded with light. Around
the table were Maxim Gorky, Andreyeva, Gorky's adopted
son, Andreyeva's daughter and son, and several other people.
Gorky wore a tan leather jacket. His hollow cheeks made the
sharp contours of his chin stand out. His long, bristly, droop-
ing mustache made him look like the military orderlies in
Russian comedies. But his intelligent eyes and the wrinkles
in his forehead attested to intense mental work. At first he
took little part in the conversation, making only brief remarks. Then he began talking abundantly and the self-taught
man appeared. He made excessive use of quotations and
scholarly terms. When he mentioned an author, he felt it necessary to introduce him. . . . Instead of saying 'Kant,' he said
'the famous philosopher Kant.' "

Cut off from the Russian land and the Russian people,
Gorky felt his creative forces diminishing. He liked Italy but,
not knowing the language of the country, he could not join in
the life of the Italian people and draw original inspiration
from them. He himself was disappointed with his *Italian
Tales*, which he wrote in Capri. Everything in those short
stories was as colorless and conventional as the comments in
a travel brochure. Lenin asked him to write for the legal magazines that the Social Democrats had recently begun publishing in St. Petersburg, outwitting the vigilance of the censors.
He also let him write for the official organ of the Bolshevik
group, the *Proletarian*, which appeared in France. In 1912,
he asked him to write either "a little tract for the first of May,
short and morally uplifting," or "a revolutionary proclama-

tion." Gorky went to Paris in April of that year, gave a lecture in the Salle Wagram and published in *L'Humanité* an open letter denouncing anti-Semitism in Russia.

These fragmentary tasks, however, did not give him the feeling that he was building a life's work. He would probably have been less dissatisfied if political action had given him a compensation for his lack of his lack of literary fervor, but although in his books and articles he celebrated the necessity of revolution, he was not deeply involved in the work of the party. To the professional Bolsheviks he was an illustrious adherent, a useful propagandist, and a respectable comrade, but they saw him as someone who fought in his own way, outside of the ranks, outside of the system, outside of discipline. Lenin and his closest companions did not suffer from living abroad because they knew it was where they could best do their underground work, which was to end with the collapse of the czarist regime. Their job was subversion, undermining; Gorky's was writing. His writing was meant for the people, of course, but it obeyed the same artistic imperatives as that of his bourgeois colleagues. Like them, or perhaps to an even greater degree, he was unable to reach his full development without going back to the sources of Russian life and deeply breathing the air of his native country. Every day he eagerly read publications that came to him from Russia, in the hope of finding an indication that the government had changed its attitude toward political émigrés. But the czar remained firm in his views. The police were still keeping a close watch on the borders. It was madness to think of going home. Gorky was overwhelmed with despair in his idyllic garden. How much longer would he have to live in the debilitating charm and solitude of Capri?

14

RETURN TO THE MOTHERLAND

In 1913, on the occasion of the three-hundredth anniversary of the Romanov dynasty, Czar Nicholas II granted a partial political amnesty that extended to violations of the laws governing the press. For Gorky, this meant that he could now go back to Russia. But maybe it was a trap. Torn between his desire to be home again and his fear of being arrested when he arrived, he hesitated and asked his friends for advice. "For writers, the amnesty seems to be total," Lenin told him. "You must try to go back to Russia, after making sure, of course, that no dirty trick will be played on you because of your 'school,' etc. But I do not think you will be bothered because of that. For a revolutionary writer, traveling inside Russia (a new Russia) means having a chance to strike a harder blow, a hundred times harder, against Romanov & Co."

In spite of this encouragement, Gorky still could not make up his mind. He was suffering from a recrudescence of his tuberculosis, and Maria felt that travel and a change of cli-

The Kashirin house where Gorky lived from 1871 to 1875. *Photo: A.P.N.*

The Volga at Nizhni Novgorod. *Photo: Viollet collection.*

Gorky. *Photo: Keystone.*

Gorky as an adolescen[
Photo: B.N.

Gorky. *Photo: B.N.*

Gorky as a young man. *Photo: Harlingue-Viollet.*

Gorky with his wife, Ekaterina Peshkov, and their children, Max and Katiusha. Nizhni Novgorod, 1903. *Photo: X.*

Gorky and his son, Max.
Photo: Roger-Viollet.

Maria Andreyeva and Gorky in
1905. *Photo: A.P.N.*

Zinovy Peshkov, Gorky's adopted
son. *Photo: Viollet collection.*

Gorky and Chekhov
at Yalta in 1900.
Photo: A.P.N.

Gorky and Tolstoy in
1900. *Photo: A.P.N.*

Stanislavsky,
Gorky, and
M. P. Lilina,
Stanislavsky's
wife, at Yalta in
1900.
Photo: A.P.N.

Gorky and Chaliapin at Nizhni Novgorod, 1902 or 1903. *Photo: A.P.N.*

Gorky, far left, and, beside him, the Italian playwright Roberto Brancco, off the coast of Capri. *Photo: Harlingue-Viollet.*

The house in Capri where Gorky lived for a long period of time. *Photo: A.P.N.*

Mutineers on the deck of the battleship *Potemkin* in 1905. *Photo: Viollet collection.*

The famine in Russia during the early years of the Revolution; a train bringing food aid. *Photo: Harlingue-Viollet.*

Russian peasants from the Baltic Provinces, 1910. *Photo: Roger-Viollet.*

Gorky's triumphal return to Russia after his long stay in Italy. *Photo: Kronika Tass.*

The cruiser *Aurora* in 1917. *Photo: A.P.N.*

Russian Revolution, 1917. Cavalry trying to stop demonstrators. *Photo: Harlingue-Viollet.*

Gorky in 1919. *Photo: Keystone.*

Gorky and Stalin. *Photo: X.*

Gorky and Lenin in 1920.
Photo: Kronika Tass.

Gorky delivering a speech in 1928 at the training camp of a military school. *Photo: A.P.N.*

Gorky speaking to a crowd in 1929. *Photo: Kronika Tass.*

Gorky among the workers of a factory in 1929. *Photo: Kronika Tass.*

"Mr. Gorky in the plastic arts."
A caricature by Efimov, 1932.
Photo: A.P.N.

Gorky toward the end of his life.
Photo: Lapi-Viollet

Romain Rolland, the French author,
and Gorky at Gorky's house near
Moscow, 1935. *Photo: A.P.N.*

Gorky in his country house near Moscow, 1935. *Photo: A.P.N.*

Left to right: Molotov, Ordzhonikidze, Stalin, and Kaganovich carrying
Gorky's ashes. *Photo: X.*

mate would be harmful to him. Informed of his relapse, Lenin also urged him to be careful: "Go to Russia in winter, from Capri? I am terribly afraid it would damage your health and destroy your ability to work. Are there first-class doctors in Italy?"

Kept away from Russia, Gorky still ardently took part in the intellectual struggles that agitated his compatriots. When he learned that the Moscow Art Theater was preparing to stage an adaptation of Dostoyevsky's *The Possessed*, an anti-revolutionary novel if ever there was one, he gave vent to his anger in an article written for the *Russian Word*: "I am deeply convinced that the propagation of Dostoyevsky's morbid ideas in the theater is capable of unsettling the already sick nerves of our society still more." This brought a violent response from Merezhkovsky, who accused him, in the same periodical, of preaching anarchy. A group of workers, however, wrote an open letter congratulating him for taking a stand against a work that "shamefully served reactionary forces."

Gorky's health gradually improved, and toward the end of 1913, he again thought seriously of returning to Russia. To be sure of impunity, he consulted his friend Chaliapin, who in spite of his leftist ideas had just regained favor with the czar and the court because of an incident that occurred while Nicholas II was attending a performance of Glinka's opera *A Life for the Czar*. When the chorus knelt on the stage before the sovereign to call their low pay and bad working conditions to his attention, Chaliapin also knelt, out of a sense of solidarity. This attitude of humility toward the czar offended most revolutionaries and even some liberals. But out of friendship for a great artist, Gorky refrained from joining in the protests. Chaliapin was grateful to him for his discretion and assured him that he could legally return to Russia without bad consequences.

At the end of December 1913, having revised the manuscript of *My Childhood*, the first volume of his autobiography, Gorky packed his suitcases. The manuscript he was taking

with him in his baggage was probably his most finished, original, and poignant work. In it, with vengeful verve, he told of
his sufferings and excitements as a child who was born into an
impoverished family and discovered life through tears,
stenches, and rage. Two other works in the same vein were to
follow: *In the World* (literal translation: *Among People*) and *My
Universities*. This trilogy showed the formation of a character
beneath the buffeting of adversity. It rang true and loud. It
alone would have been enough to ensure Gorky's survival as a
writer.

As soon as he set foot on Russian soil, he was under police
surveillance. The head of the Okhrana in St. Petersburg immediately notified the head of the police department that, on
December 31, his agents had "begun shadowing the well-
known émigré... Alexey Maximovich Peshkov, who, it appears, arrived on a train coming from the border station of
Verzhbolovo." But Gorky was not arrested, probably because
it was feared that arresting him would turn him into a martyr.

His return was greeted enthusiastically by all adversaries of
the regime. Sympathetic messages came to him from all over
Russia. Students in Moscow wrote to him, "You have now
come back among us, just before our awakening from a long,
wearisome sleep. . . . We firmly hope that we are about to see
the blossoming of springtime, and we like to believe that we
will welcome it with you." Groups of workers expressed the
same confidence in him: "We are certain that your return to
the motherland and your spiritual influence will increase our
strength and help us, the Russian proletariat, to throw off the
sinister yoke of czarism."

Tired from travel and illness, and advised by Chaliapin,
who begged him not to attract the attention of the police,
Gorky refused to attend meetings that young people wanted to
hold in his honor; and instead of living in St. Petersburg or
Moscow, he withdrew to the village of Moustamiaki, in Finland, near the Russian border.

Being far away from the capital did not prevent him from

having close relations with revolutionary circles. As in Capri, he received many visitors and was nearly buried under an avalanche of letters and manuscripts. On this subject he wrote, in this preface to *The Enchanted Grass*, a book by the peasant Ivan Morozov, "Each time the mail brings me a gray notebook of cheap paper covered with clumsy handwriting and accompanied by a letter in which someone unknown but familiar, invisible but close, asks me to 'look over' his essays and tell him if he has any talent, if he has a right to attention, I feel joy in my heart. . . . I sense that in the lower levels of society people are becoming more aware of the bond that attaches them to the world, that they yearn more and more ardently for a broad, vast life, for freedom."

But in the midst of all his mingled political and literary activities, he felt growing anxiety over the future. To be close to the focus of social unrest, he took an apartment on the Kronversky Prospekt in St. Petersburg. From then on, he divided his time between the capital and his house in the country.

In 1913, Gorky had written in an article published in the *Russian Word*, "No one can deny that clouds are again gathering over Russia, promising great storms." The "storm" did not break until the following year: the assassination, in Sarajevo, of Archduke Franz Ferdinand, heir to the crown of Austria-Hungary; Vienna's ultimatum to Serbia; panic in Western embassies; the interaction of alliances; Russian and Austrian mobilization; and, on July 19, 1914 (August 1 by the Gregorian calendar), Germany's declaration of war against Russia. The next day, Gorky announced, "One thing is clear: we are entering the first act of a worldwide tragedy."

World War I caused a deep division within the Social Revolutionary and Social Democratic parties. One faction—following Plekhanov, the spiritual father of Russian Marxism; Vera Zasulich and Leo Deutsch, founders of Russian social democracy; and Kropotkin, the anarchist leader—unconditionally advocated defending Russia against German imperialism. They were called "social patriots" by Lenin and his associates Zinovyev and Bukharin, who preferred "defeatism" and were counting on a German victory, which, they believed, would bring about a revolution in Russia.

After hesitating for several days, Gorky wholeheartedly sided with the "defeatists." His hatred of czarism, his contempt of the army, his conviction that wars were fomented by governments while peoples only wanted peace—because of all this, he ridiculed the patriotic passion that made masses rally around Nicholas II as soon as the opening of hostilities was announced. He was alarmed and appalled to see how the threat of foreign invasion produced a sudden love of the nation for its sovereign; to him it was like an outbreak of collective insanity. All at once the czar's crimes were forgotten and crowds joined in fervent communion before icons and the flag. The Germans were monsters and the Russians were innocent lambs. The German-sounding name of St. Petersburg was changed to the more Russian name of Petrograd.

In his fury against patriots, Gorky broke off all relations with his adopted son, Zinovy Peshkov, who was then in France. Zinovy became a naturalized French citizen, enrolled in the French army, was wounded, and had to have his right arm amputated.[1] Unable to write, he asked the revolutionary Grigory Alexinsky, who had come to visit him at the American hospital in Neuilly, to send Gorky a letter telling him what had happened. Gorky replied to Alexinsky that he was sorry to learn that his adopted son had lost an arm in "an imperialist war." "His letter was so harsh and curt," Alexinsky later wrote, "that I preferred not to show it to his son."

Gorky must have been proud to sacrifice his fatherly affection to his revolutionary principles. In doing so, he felt that he had the stern soul of an ancient Roman. But his defeatism was actually much less strict than Lenin's. Although he condemned the war, he could not bring himself to say openly that he wanted the enemy to win.

In 1915, he collected funds to publish a magazine, the *Chronicle*, in Petrograd, with himself as its editor. The source of the funds was mysterious. It was rumored that they came from a Germanophile banker named Manus, who advocated a Russian-German alliance, or from Rizov, the Bulgarian ambassador to Berlin. But Gorky cared nothing about those accusations. He felt that any means of undermining morale on the home front was justified. He had to make sure, however, that he did not upset the censors. He meted out his venom in small doses. Sometimes he even departed from Lenin's directives. This timid "deviationism" often made Gorky the target of criticism from the Bolsheviks, especially since Bogdanov and several comrades from Gorky's days in Capri acted as a brake in the editorial staff of the *Chronicle*. They went so far as to water down the prose of Lenin himself. When he outwitted police surveillance and managed to have an article for the magazine smuggled in from abroad, they respectfully asked him to make changes in it. Outraged, Lenin wrote, "I was able to have my manuscript on imperialism get through to Petersburg, and now I've been told that the editor (it's Gorky, that silly fool!) is unhappy about my charges against—against whom do you think?—against Kautsky!"[2] He also wrote in a letter to Shlyapnikov in 1916, "In politics, Gorky has always shown a total lack of character; he gives in to his feelings and moods."

Gorky, meanwhile, continued his soft-spoken propaganda. Around him, the government was arresting his comrades, imprisoning them, sending them to Siberia. Every morning he woke up in fear that his home might be searched. But, far from making him disheartened, anger strengthened his convictions. "On the whole, the atmosphere is unbreatheable," he wrote on June 10, 1915, to Malyshev, who had just been deported. "I have never before felt so necessary to Russian life, and it has been a long time since I felt such courage in myself, but, dear comrade, I recognize that sometimes my arms fall and a veil darkens my sight. . . . Yet I am succeeding to some extent. I am succeeding mainly because the Petersburg proletariat furnishes people who are all first-rate."

And in the midst of the war he said, in an article written for his magazine, "The press must keep repeating to people that any war—except for the war against stupidity—is a disaster comparable to cholera." The article was forbidden by the censors.

During this period he published the first two volumes of his autobiography, *My Childhood* and *In the World*, in the *Chronicle*. He also induced many famous writers to publish in the magazine, including Korolenko, Bunin, Blok, Yesenin, Lunacharsky, and Mayakovsky. He was especially enthusiastic about Mayakovsky. "There is no futurism in him," he said, as quoted in Yurkovsky's diary. "There is only Mayakovsky in him! A poet. A great poet."

Despite the excellence of the people who wrote for the magazine, Lenin, still in exile, continued to regard it as "deeply suspect." Undiscouraged, Gorky created a publishing house called The Sail, whose activities were intended to enlighten the people on their political future. The reactionary newspapers relentlessly attacked the *Chronicle* and The Sail, but the government tolerated those two bastions of antibourgeois thought, while keeping them under close police surveillance.

Although they were played down in official communiqués, the first Russian reverses on the front alarmed the public. Badly commanded, equipped, and supplied, the Russian soldiers fought the Germans heroically but in vain. Casualties were enormous. All hospitals were packed full of wounded men. Those who came back from the inferno at the front denounced the generals' incompetence and talked openly about the uselessness of that butchery. The tide of Slavophile euphoria was rapidly ebbing. The need for political change was already being discussed in drawing rooms. Some liberals were even considering the possibility of a separate peace. The czar was reviled for letting his best subjects be slaughtered to relieve the French army, and the czarina for being totally under the influence of the dissolute Rasputin and the clique of inept grand dukes. Maybe they should all be brought back to their senses. Maybe the czar should even be forced to abdicate. . . . Another czar? A constitutional monarchy? A republic with a transitional government that would continue the war on the side of the Allies? There was no agreement on what should be done.

"We will soon have a famine," Gorky wrote to Ekaterina on November 30, 1915. "I advise you to buy ten pounds of bread and hide it. In the environs of Petrograd, well-dressed women can be seen begging. It is very cold. People have nothing to burn in their stoves. Here and there, at night, they tear down wooden fences. . . . You meet a horribly large number of underage prostitutes. On your way home at night, you see them scurrying along the sidewalks like cockroaches, blue with cold and starving. Last Tuesday I talked to one of them. I put some money into her hand and hurried away, in tears, in such a state of sorrow that I felt like banging my head against a wall."

In 1916, strikes became more frequent. Peasants began looting aristocratic estates. In the cities, people lined up at dawn in front of bakeries, grocery stores, and butchers' shops. With their stocks gone in the twinkling of an eye, the shopkeepers closed their iron shutters. A few shops were broken open. At the front, soldiers were deserting by the thousands. "People live from one fear to the next," Gorky wrote to Timiriazev on October 16, 1915. "Their hatred of each other increases savagely, while respect for humanity diminishes more and more." And to Ekaterina in late February 1916, "My heart is heavy, Ekaterina. I have never been inclined to complain, but now I am complaining. My heart is heavy. These are terrible times; people are loathsome, everything is rotting, no one knows how to work any more, no one understands the value of work."

He passionately followed the phases in the decomposition

of the empire. But he still did not dare to believe that his dream was so close to coming true. The joy aroused in the public by the assassination of Rasputin, the violent intervention of the Left in the Duma, the insistence of some generals that the czar be relieved of supreme command of the army— these were signs that the great revolutionary festival was approaching.

In February 1917, massive uprisings of workers in Petrograd, Moscow, and most other Russian cities brought about the creation of a provisional government headed by Prince Lvov. Most of his colleagues, including Kerensky, were progressives. They demanded that the czar abdicate and that the crown prince take the throne under the regency of Grand Duke Michael. But Gorky could still see no way out of that political commotion. It did not seem to him that a strong, coherent popular regime could ever arise from anarchy. "I do not believe in a revolutionary army," he wrote to Ekaterina on March 1, "I think that lack of discipline and organization is mistaken for revolutionary spirit. All the regiments in Petersburg have sided with the Duma, but the officers, up to a certain point, are on the side of Rodzianko and Milyukov.[3] Only visionary minds can expect the army to support the Soviet of workers' deputies. The police, hidden in attics, shoot at the crowd and the soldiers with machine guns. Automobiles full of soldiers drive around the city with red flags; they are looking for policemen in civilian clothes, to arrest them. Sometimes they kill them, but usually they take them to the Duma. . . . In all that, there is more absurdity than greatness. Looting has begun. What will come of this situation? I have no idea. We will not go back, but we will not go forward very much. And, of course, there will be much bloodshed, an incredible amount."

On March 2, the czar, at the urging of the politicians and generals, and some members of his family, finally gave up the crown in favor of his brother, Grand Duke Michael. But, fearing another outbreak of turmoil if he accepted the crown,

Michael refused it and exhorted the nation to submit to the provisional government. Thus Russia ceased to be an empire. Despite the importance of that change, Gorky remained skeptical. The new rulers of the country were liberals, bourgeois. Would they be able to end the war? He hoped so with all his heart, but he was also afraid that the people, exhilarated by their first successes, might engage in violence. His respect for humanity and culture was such that he preferred even a moderate government to savage disorder in the streets. He did not want the butchery between Russians and Germans to be followed by butchery among Russians. Anything would be better than a dictatorship of terror.

This prudent attitude was not to the liking of the Bolsheviks, who, with Lenin, preached the negation of old values and the liquidation of opponents. Carrying their reasoning through to the end, they hoped for chaos from which a new society would emerge; whereas Gorky, wavering between theory and practice, loudly voiced his love of the people and at the same time feared the excesses of the blind, cruel masses. In his books he had so often denounced the dull-witted brutality of those masses—and so often exalted the value of civilization, education, and art—that he was now on the verge of condemning himself for having sided with tyranny.

15

THE REVOLUTION

E vents were moving swiftly. Each day added to the disorder of the day before. Soldiers abandoned their barracks and loitered in the streets. Mountains of garbage rose on the sidewalks and no one was willing to take them away. Demonstrators paraded between them, preceded by red flags. Committees and subcommittees flourished in all administrations and enterprises. Public meetings were held at the drop of a hat, anywhere. It was a time of verbiage and confusion. The czar and the imperial family were interned at Tsarskoye Selo. The Petrograd garrison was assured that, because of its loyalty to the revolutionary cause, it would not be sent to the front. As one political crisis followed another, Kerensky acquired decisive importance in the government. A lawyer and a bombastic, grimacing demagogue, he piled up promises and threats and became intoxicated with the sound of his own voice.

On April 3, 1917, Lenin arrived in Petrograd. He had

come from Switzerland and crossed Germany in a sealed railroad car, traveling in wartime with the consent of the German authorities. A crowd of soldiers and workers cheered him when he got off the train. He immediately set about making preparations for an armed insurrection.

Aware of the danger of such an explosion of violence, Gorky published in the *Chronicle* an article denouncing the Bolsheviks' extremist tendencies: "We must remember that we are living in the jungle of a mass composed of millions and millions of practically illiterate and socially uneducated people. . . . People who do not know what they want are politically and socially dangerous." And he advised seeking "a common ground on which men can understand each other. This common ground," he said, "is the development of science. Science must become democratic. It must be made accessible to all the people." He stressed the need for an alliance between the working-class elite and the liberal intelligentsia of scientists, artists, and technicians, and he upheld that idea with redoubled vigor in *New Life*, the daily newspaper he had just founded. Seeing the turbulence around him, he asked his compatriots to "go to work for the general development of culture," protested against the "idiocy and cruelty" of certain summary executions, and stigmatized "people who try to prove something with bullets, bayonets, or punches in the face." He even went so far as to condemn the circulation of coarse and "pornographic" brochures that cast aspersions on the czar, the czarina, and their entourage. It seemed to him that such sordid writings were dangerous at the time when "dark instincts" were being aroused.

In another article, dated May 31, he made his point more forcefully: "Creeping along the streets like venomous, hissing snakes, newspapers poison and terrify the average man by teaching him a so-called 'freedom of speech,' which in this case is actually freedom to slander and distort the truth. 'Free speech' becomes indecent speech." Soon afterward, on June 9, he added, "Every day [the press] instills the most shameful feelings—malice, deceitfulness, hypocrasy, cynicism—into its readers' minds. ... And to think that the revolution was initiated precisely in the interest of culture!" This concern with safeguarding the values of civilization made Trotsky, Lenin's closest collaborator, say with contemptuous irony, "Gorky has greeted the revolution with the anxiety of a museum curator. He is truly horrified by soldiers in retreat and workers who are not working."

While Gorky was busily making appeals to reason, brotherhood, and respect for science—and saying, "It seems to me that the cry 'The motherland is in danger!' is less frightening than the cry 'Culture is in danger!'"—Lenin was fomenting a large-scale revolt against the provisional government. It broke out on July 3 and ended in failure, for lack of preparation. Led by Bolsheviks, the demonstrators demanded that the government be dissolved and that power be turned over to the Petrograd Soviet, a council of workers' and soldiers' delegates that was constantly in session. But the moderate majority in the Soviet had no desire to take on that responsibility. That night, regiments loyal to Kerensky drove away the rioters who were still in the streets. Several Bolshevik leaders were imprisoned. Lenin was able to flee in disguise.

On July 14, Gorky condemned that failed revolution, calling it an "ignominious tragedy" and a symbol of "heavy Russian imbecility." Less than a week later he was expressing indignation at the way some journalists had been attacking the czarina, who was sick and in captivity. "Jeering at someone ill and miserable is despicable," he proclaimed. Feeling that the Bolsheviks were preparing for another uprising, he wrote in his column for October 18, "This means that we will again see trucks full of people holding rifles and pistols and trembling with fear; it means that those guns will be fired into storefronts, at passersby, anywhere. ... A disorganized crowd of people who do not know what they want will move through the streets, and among them will be adventurers, thieves, professional killers. ... In short, we will see a repetition of the

senseless, bloody slaughter we have already known, which
has destroyed the revolution's moral conception and cultural
meaning all over the country."

His mistrust of Bolshevik machinations did not prevent him
from constantly vilifying, in *New Life*, the French and British
capitalists and imperialists who, he maintained, were solely
responsible for the war. Indignant at his repeated attacks,
Charles de Chambrun, first secretary of the French embassy,
paid him a visit to complain about them and found him sitting
at his desk, looking sickly and distraught. "I was struck by
his broad forehead," he wrote. "Three wrinkles engraved his
troubles in it, and the third one joined his disheveled eye-
brows. How sad his eyes were!... He gave the impression of
being a strange, apathetic man who had been pampered too
late and had seen his genius, tamed and repressed by well-
being, abandon him. Genius does not like luxury."

When Charles de Chambrun complained to Gorky about
the campaign of abuse he was waging against France in his
newspaper, Gorky replied that his articles must have been
mistranslated, that he regarded France "as his mother," but
that he could not bear the thought of that "cursed war," that
"infamous butchery." "Stop fighting," he said in conclusion.
"Russia is big enough to give Germany a larger province in
exchange for the one you're dreaming of. What difference
does territory make? Only human happiness matters." The
"beautiful Madame Andreyeva" was present during the conversation, "with her captivating smile," and also Gorky's
adopted son, Lieutenant Zinovy Peshkov, who had come from
France to accompany the diplomat. He listened to his foster
father with intense emotion. "I looked at Gorky," wrote
Charles de Chambrun, "and he seemed to be feeling sorry for
me, himself, and his son Peshkov." Maria Andreyeva served
tea with cakes and honey. Then Gorky wrote a dedication to
Zinovy in one of his books, showed his visitors to the door,
and said, "Let's forget our differences of opinion; they're un-
important." In the street, Zinovy read the dedication: "To my

tenderly loved son who has become—is it possible?—a chauvinistic Frenchman."[1]

Meanwhile, at the front, the Russian offensive demanded by the Kerensky government had turned into a disaster. Disheartened by the prospect of a fourth winter campaign in mud, snow, and cold, soldiers were abandoning their positions and forcing their way into trains to go home. Most factories were on strike. Whole villages were nearly wiped out by famine. Lenin, who had clandestinely returned from Finland, saw that circumstances were favorable for a general insurrection and ordered that hostilities be opened on October 25, 1917. Bolshevik commissars went to barracks and arsenals to call on soldiers and workers to obey only decisions made by the Soviet. Imperial emblems were demolished and trampled underfoot everywhere; there was a massacre of double-headed eagles.

In response to the uprising, the Kerensky government gathered in the Winter Palace and mustered several more or less reliable regiments. After ten hours of fighting, most strategic points were in the hands of the rebels. The cruiser *Aurora*, anchored in the Neva, fired blank charges in the direction of the Winter Palace, shaking the chandeliers in the room where the provisional government had gathered. Kerensky fled in a car with a British flag, to look for hypothetical reinforcements outside the city. The horde of rebels stormed the majestic building, now defended only by a few cadets and women soldiers. The ministers were arrested and taken to the Peter and Paul Fortress. The Bolsheviks' victory was complete. And Lenin, having been appointed president of the Council of People's Commissars, had absolute power.

Gorky, however, still continued to express his misgivings about the victors' political orientation. He declared himself to be a staunch socialist, but he wrote in *New Life* on November 7, "Lenin, Trotsky, and their fellow travelers have already been poisoned by the slimy venom of power. It can be seen in their shameful attitude toward freedom of speech, individual freedom, and all the rights for which democracy has struggled. . . . Blind fanatics and unscrupulous adventurers are hurrying along the path of the so-called 'social revolution,' but that path actually leads to anarchy, a mortal danger for the proletariat and the revolution. On that path, Lenin and his comrades in arms believe that any crime is justified; for example, the fighting near Petersburg and the massacres in Moscow, suppression of freedom of speech, senseless arrests, and all sorts of ignominious acts comparable to those committed by Plehve and Stolypin. . . . The working class cannot fail to understand that Lenin is performing an experiment with their flesh and blood, that he is trying to raise the revolutionary spirit to its highest degree, to see what will result from it. . . . Lenin is not an all-powerful sorcerer, he is an impassive conjurer who does not spare the proletariat's honor or life. The workers must not allow adventurers and lunatics to hold the proletariat accountable for shameful, senseless, and bloody crimes; it is not Lenin who will pay for those crimes but the proletariat itself. . . . Lenin's power arrests and imprisons everyone who does not share his ideas, as the Romanovs' power used to do. . . . Sensible democratic elements must decide if they want to go on traveling along this road with plotters and anarchists."

And three days later, "Lenin's supporters, imagining that they are Napoleons of socialism, are frenziedly finishing up the process of destroying Russia, and the Russian people will pay for it with lakes of blood. . . . Lenin is a gifted man who has all the qualities of a leader, including these essential ones: lack of morality and a merciless, lordly harshness toward the lives of the masses. Lenin is a leader and a Russian nobleman; the psychological traits of that vanished social class are not foreign to him, and that is why he believes himself authorized to use the Russian people in a cruel experiment that is sure to fail. The people, exhausted and ruined by the war, have already paid for that experiment with tens of thousands of human lives, and they will be forced to pay tens of thousands more, which will leave the country decapitated for a long time. This inevitable tragedy does not trouble Lenin, a slave of dogma, or his acolytes, slaves of their leader. Life in its complexity does not interest him, he does not know the masses, he has not lived among them; but he has learned from books how to make those masses rebel, and how to develop their savage instincts. The working class is to Lenin what ore is to a smelter. . . . What does Lenin risk if the experiment fails? He works like a chemist in his laboratory, with this difference: the chemist uses inert matter and his effort gives a result that benefits life, while Lenin works with living matter and leads the revolution toward destruction. The clear-headed workers who follow Lenin must realize that an experiment is being performed on the Russian working class that will annihilate the workers' vigor and stop the normal development of the revolution for a long time."

The Bolshevik press responded to these repeated attacks by accusing Gorky of having "taken off his mask" and of "betraying the people after serving democracy for twenty years." Gorky haughtily replied in *New Life*, on November 12, 1917, "Those Bolshevik gentlemen have a right to describe my attitude as they please, but I must remind them that I have never been blinded by the beautiful qualities of the Russian people's soul and that I have never knelt before democracy, which I do not regard as something too sacred to be criticized. . . . I cannot march in the ranks of that fraction of the working class, which, incited by demented masters, shows class consciousness by using violence and terror. . . . It is shameful and criminal that people who refuse to join in Mr. Trotsky's wild dance on the ruins of Russia should be frightened with acts of terror and pogroms!"

And it was true that, at the prompting of the recently created secret-police organization known as the Cheka, house searches, arrests, hostage-taking, and summary executions were increasing at an enormous rate. No one was safe from a neighbor's denunciation. Anyone suspected of liberal opinions was treated as an enemy of the people. Whole families disappeared, from one day to the next. Gorky himself no longer felt safe. But he intensified his efforts to make the new leaders of the country take a more humane attitude. He was so persistent that *Pravda*, the official organ of the Bolshevik Central Committee, openly accused him of "speaking the language of the enemies of the working class" and even wondered if that writer who had "so hurriedly left the ranks of revolutionary democracy" would be a "desirable guest at the glittering festival of peoples and peace."

Gorky's rejoinder was immediate and sharp: "I want no part of a festival in which the despotism of a semiliterate mass celebrates its easy victory while the human personality remains oppressed, as before. That is not a festival for me. No matter whose hands hold power, I reserve my human right to criticize. And it is with particular suspicion and mistrust that I consider the Russian man when he is in power: having been a slave only yesterday, he becomes the most ruthless of despots as soon as he feels that he is the master of his fellow men."

On December 6, analyzing the causes of Russian stagnation, he wrote, "This cursed war has exterminated tens of thousands of the best Russian workers, and the people who have replaced them at their machines to work for 'national defense' have done so only to escape being drafted into the army. They are all alien to proletarian psychology, have no political understanding, and are not attracted by the idea of building a new culture. They are animated only by the bourgeois desire to ensure their material welfare as quickly as possible, at all costs. They are constitutionally incapable of accepting and carrying out the ideas of a pure socialism."

The next day, he indignantly denounced arbitrary executions, the lynching of suspects, the crude arrogance of the People's Commissars, who had the right of life and death over all citizens. Three days later he wrote, in the same paper, "The People's Commissars are ruining and destroying the

working class in Russia. . . . As long as I can, I will repeat to
the Russian proletariat, 'You are being led to destruction, you
are being used as material in an inhuman experiment; to your
leaders, you are not human.'"

On December 22, the threats hanging over *New Life* became more specific: there was talk of its being banned immediately. But Gorky still refused to back down: "Yes, we will go
on criticizing a government that is leading the working class
to destruction; we consider it to be our duty, the duty of honest citizens and independent socialists."

On December 24, he published a Christmas article in
which he said, "Yes, yes, we are living in blood and filth up
to our necks, and thick clouds of ignoble coarseness surround
us and blind many of us." And he added this profession of
faith which must have given Lenin a jolt: "Today is Christ's
birthday. . . . Christ, the immortal idea of mercy and love, and
Prometheus, enemy of the gods, the first rebel against fate—
humanity has created nothing greater than those two symbols
of its highest aspirations. . . . Heartfelt greetings to everyone
who feels isolated in the storm of events! . . . Heartfelt greetings to everyone being unjustly held in prison!" For New
Year's Day he once again spoke of the terrible present time in
which people, "deafened by propaganda extolling equality
and brotherhood, rob their fellow citizens in the streets." He
even declared, "The Russian man is bad, worse than he has
ever been before."

In February 1918, the separate peace concluded in the
Treaty of Brest-Litovsk strongly displeased the editorial staff
of *New Life*. Negotiated by Trotsky, it recognized Germany's
seizure of Poland and the Baltic Provinces and restored some
parts of the Caucasus to Turkey. *New Life* published a sharply
critical article by Sukhanov, titled "The Surrender." To the
government of the Soviets, this was the last straw. The paper
was suspended for a week. As soon as it resumed publication,
Gorky continued his fight against the new Russia, "stinking,
dirty, drunk, and cruel." On March 4, 1918, he deplored the

passing of a time "when the nation had a conscience, when even the most obscure people in the provinces confusedly felt a yearning for social justice in their souls." "In our nightmarish time," he went on, "conscience is dead. . . . Six innocent students are shot, dozens of 'bourgeois' are slaughtered in Sebastopol and Yevpatoriya, and no one thinks to ask the leaders of the social revolution if they are not the spiritual instigators of those mass murders."

In June, the paper was again suspended, for several days. Then on July 16, by Lenin's order, *New Life* ceased to exist. (Gorky's articles in it were later published separately, under the title *Untimely Thoughts.*)

However great his respect for Gorky's talent and personality, Lenin could no longer tolerate his calls for indulgence toward liberal intellectuals and his denunciations of the barbarity of the masses. The stiffening of his attitude was explained by the need to mobilize the whole nation against the "White Army" organized by former czarist generals. Volunteers from all over the country were swelling the ranks of the Bolsheviks' adversaries. The Soviets were in desperate straits. Under those conditions, there was no longer any room for shades of opinion within the revolutionary spirit. Hesitations, misgivings, and qualms of conscience amounted to betrayal. "In the present circumstances," Lenin said at a public meeting, "when it is important to rouse the nation to defend the revolution, all intellectual pessimism is harmful. Gorky is our man. . . . He will come back to us. . . . He has already gone through such political zigzags before." Thus, while depriving Gorky of his public platform, Lenin made it plain that there were to be no personal attacks on him.

By now, Gorky himself was not far from thinking that he had gone a little astray in his anger against the Bolsheviks. The strange shift that would turn the rebel into a conformist was already beginning inside him. This metamorphosis, which astounded some of the people close to him, resulted not from a sudden ideological revelation but from a series of small resignations. The failure of his opposition to Bolshevik tyranny had finally convinced him that any further struggle would be futile. Tired of rowing against the current, he discovered the psychological and material benefits of opportunism. There was nothing to be gained, he thought, from denying everyday reality. And so, without fully subscribing to Bolshevik doctrine, he moved closer to those who were its most vigorous supporters. It was not yet submission, but a kind of ambiguous accommodation. He had not become a turncoat, he was only marching in step. In July 1918, he wrote to Ekaterina, "I am preparing to work with the Bolsheviks on an autonomous basis. I have had enough of the academic, powerless opposition of *New Life*."

In March 1918, the capital was transferred from Petrograd to Moscow. In July, the czar and his family were killed in Ekaterinburg (now Sverdlovsk). Now, in accordance with Lenin's wishes, nothing was left of the execrated czarist regime. But on August 30, Lenin himself was wounded in an assassination attempt. The next day, Gorky and his companion Maria Andreyeva sent him a telegram: "Terribly distressed and worried, we wholeheartedly wish you a quick recovery. Be firm in your soul." Then Gorky went to visit Lenin in the Kremlin. He found him still weak from his wound, but smiling and sure of final victory. Before him, as before a priest of an unquestionable religion, Gorky confessed his doubts and errors. Lenin replied cordially, "Anyone who's not with us is against us. Tell the intellectuals to join us." Soon afterward, on October 6, the *Red Gazette* triumphantly announced, "The working class welcomes the return of its beloved son. Maxim Gorky is again one of us. He has come back and, silently and invisibly, has begun helping in the work of his father, the Russian proletariat."

Gorky's son Max, now twenty-one, had become an active Bolshevik who, unlike his father, had no moral misgivings. He was the adjutant of the commandant of the Kremlin, worked for the Cheka, and often saw Lenin in Moscow. When he wanted to join the Red Army to fight the Whites, Lenin said to him, "Your place is with your father. You must take care of him and protect him."

Gorky tenderly loved his son. Whenever he had an outburst of anger against the regime, Max's enthusiastic words would calm him temporarily. At the end of 1919, he wrote to Ekaterina, "Maxim firmly believes that life can and must be transformed with the means used by the Soviet regime, and in accordance with its directives. I don't believe that. . . . At his age, feeling oneself associated with the process of creating a new life is a great joy, unknown to you and me and, in general, to our generation. I know what you are afraid of: we will all perish, inevitably, crushed by the peasantry. The Western proletariat has betrayed the Russian workers, and the Western bourgeoisie will support the Russian peasants in their victory over the city."

Driven by this fear, he continued to struggle, by words and charitable acts, against the excesses of the unbridled populace. The public man in him was devouring the private man. Wanting to raise the morale of the troops, he gave speeches even to the militiamen, praising their vigilance and acts of repression. "Between you and the policemen of the czarist regime," he said to them on March 11, 1920, "there is an enormous difference. The policeman of the past was concerned less with making order reign in the streets than with making it reign in people's minds, and trying to bend thought from left to right. You, however, must be good comrades. But you must not forget that there is still one category of harmful individuals: enemies of discipline."

The whole country was on the brink of total collapse. Winter proved to be cruel. Ink froze in inkwells. People slept with all their clothes on. Meager food rations were distributed every two weeks. Bringing home a chunk of bread meant waiting in line for hours. The sidewalks, covered with ice, were unusable. No more streetcars, no more automobiles, only pedestrians cautiously walking in the middle of the pavement. If a horse fell in the street, a crowd gathered around him to wait for his death and cut him into pieces. Since all plumbing had frozen, toilets could no longer be used. Buckets of excrement were dumped in courtyards or in front of buildings. Well-dressed gentlemen urinated on the Nevsky Prospekt in Petrograd. "Men became impotent, women stopped menstruating," noted the writer Viktor Shklovsky. "People died simply, and at a more rapid rate. For a burial, the common procedure was to find a sled, call on a friend or relative for help, get a coffin, sometimes by renting it, and pull the body to the cemetery."

In the midst of this disaster, Gorky refused to lose hope. He organized a committee to protect museums, art objects, and historical monuments. In the name of the committee, he appealed to his compatriots: "Preserve paintings, statues, and buildings: they are embodiments of your spiritual power and that of your forefathers. Art is the beauty that talented people have been able to create, even under the yoke of despotism." He also did his best to help intellectuals, whose situation under the Soviet regime had become tragic. Forgetting the self-taught man's rancor against an elite too proud of its knowledge, he made impassioned efforts to save writers, teachers, artists, and technicians from the clutches of the Cheka, which regarded them as suspect. Since most of them were starving, he tried to get bread and sugar for them. On his recommendation, some of them were given "academic rations." Actors, singers, and musicians, chosen by him, performed in "workers' clubs" and "Red Guard clubs" in exchange for a little food.

In spite of Gorky's intercessions, about a hundred scientists, some of them among the most famous in the world, died of hunger and hardship. Others were coldly "liquidated" for their bourgeois ideas. "Scientists who oppose Bolshevik power," said Lunacharsky, the People's Commissar of Education, "cannot claim personal inviolability, whatever their scientific achievements may be." Of the 1.7 million prisoners shot by the Cheka in the early years of the revolution, 350,000 were intellectuals.

That methodical extermination made Gorky frantic. He was always ready to intercede with the Soviet authorities in behalf of someone in trouble. From morning to night, his apartment was assailed by people who wanted his help. Those who came there to beg did not always share his ideas. Tormented by hunger, they humbled themselves to survive. Gorky knew it. Did it embarrass him? Maybe not. His personal victory made him doubly generous to those hounded and humiliated men and women. "People came there for all sorts of affairs," wrote the poet Khodasevich, "from the 'House of Art,' the 'House of Writers,' the 'House of Scholars,' the 'Institute of World Literature'; there were writers and scientists from St. Petersburg and elsewhere, workers, sailors, artists, painters, speculators, former courtiers, society ladies. He was asked to intercede for prisoners; through him, one could obtain food rations, housing, clothes, medicine, railroad tickets, tobacco, paper, ink, false teeth for old people, milk for babies — in short, everything it was impossible to get without influence. Gorky listened to everyone and wrote countless letters of recommendation."

For Gorky, playing the part of a socialist Santa Claus was both exhilarating and exhausting. He himself lacked nothing: his food was abundant, his apartment well heated. "A friend of Lenin," wrote the painter Yuri Annenkov, "Gorky belonged to the category of 'beloved comrades,' founders of the new privileged class. 'Beloved comrades' lived very comfortably. They lived even better than before the revolution. . . . Gorky's bedroom and study were full of statuettes of Buddha and polychromatic Chinese lacquers. He avidly collected them. . . . One curious detail: in that 'Marxist's' library, whose shelves were packed with books concerning all cultural orientations, I never found (though I looked carefully) a single volume of the works of Karl Marx. He had nicknamed Marx 'Karlushka' and he called Lenin 'the pretty nobleman.'"

Victor Serge, a revolutionary who visited Gorky during this period, was also struck by the comfort of his apartment, "warm as a greenhouse" and filled with books and Chinese art objects. "He himself was chilly even under his thick gray sweater," wrote Serge, "and coughed terribly, the result of his thirty years' struggle against tuberculosis. Tall, lean and bony, broad-shouldered and hollow-chested, he stooped a little as he walked. His frame, sturdily-built but anaemic, appeared essentially as a support for his head, an ordinary, Russian man-in-the-street's head, bony and pitted, really almost ugly with its jutting cheek-bones, great thin-lipped mouth and professional smeller's nose, broad and peaked. His complexion deathly, he was chewing away under his short, bristly moustache, full of dejection, or rather of anguish mingled with indignation. His bushy brows puckered readily, and his big, grey eyes held an extraordinary wealth of expression. . . . He spoke harshly about the Bolsheviks: they were 'drunk with authority,' 'cramping the violent, spontaneous anarchy of the Russian people,' and 'starting bloody despotism all over again'; all the same they were 'facing chaos alone' with some incorruptible men in their leadership. . . . The fate of the hostages in the jails was nothing short of monstrous. Hunger was weakening the masses, and distorting the cerebral processes of the whole country."[2]

After a meeting with Gorky in the home of mutual friends, the writer Zinaida Hippius, wife of Merezhkovsky, noted in her diary, "He [Gorky] made a frightful impression on me. He is somber, gloomy. . . . When he talks, it's as if he were quietly barking. He refuses to solicit anything from the [Bolshevik] ministers. 'I can't talk to that riffraff, Lenin and Trotsky,' he says. 'It's a visceral reaction.'" When Zinaida Hippius told him that none of his articles in *New Life* really distinguished him from Lenin and the Bolsheviks, and that he ought to break off from those people, he replied in a hoarse voice, "Leave them? But whom would I go with then?" And, taking advantage of another visitor's arrival, he walked away from her, "somber, stooped, tormented, unhappy, and intimidating."

Gorky's efforts to intercede with Lenin and his collaborators were not always successful. When he was unable to help people, they often resented his failure and accused him of working hand in glove with the merciless Bolshevik regime. The fact was, however, that although the regime treated him gently, it regarded him as "unreliable." Lenin forgave his verbal outbursts, his "political zigzags," as he said ironically, but his entourage, particularly Kamenev and Zinovyev, kept an eye on him. This did not bother Gorky and, in spite of his equivocal situation, he continued his agitation and thunderous denunciations.

At the end of 1918 he had taken part in creating the first workers' and peasants' university. He published the works of young writers. He, the man without diplomas, taught courses on the history of civilization in the mobile university for workers and sailors of the Red Fleet. As for the rare and valuable art objects he collected, he did not care too much about their origin. Quite a few of them came from the looting of bourgeois apartments.

His companion, Maria Andreyeva, had obtained an official post. In 1919, she was already People's Commissar for the Theater and People's Commissar for Foreign Trade. Later she was placed in charge of liquidating "surplus artistic valuables"—that is, of selling abroad, for foreign currency, art objects confiscated by the Soviets in the course of house searches.[3] This activity aroused the indignation of some liberal writers, who accused Gorky of helping to dissipate the Russian national heritage and living in scandalous comfort while so many members of the intelligentsia were dying of hunger and cold.

Lenin was becoming more and more irritated by the interventions of his "favorite author" in behalf of scholars, writers, and artists at a time when White volunteers were trying to dislodge the Bolshevik troops from their positions all along

the front. No sooner had the Red Army triumphed over Kras-
nov's soldiers than Kolchak's regiments were deployed on the
Volga. When Kolchak had been driven back into Siberia,
Denikin approached the center with sizable forces. Petrograd
itself was threatened. From Moscow, Max wrote to his father
in May 1919, "Here, the situation of Petrograd is not con-
cealed from us, and the possibility that the city may be abandoned [to the Whites] for a time is not ruled out. . . . If
Petrograd falls, your situation will be horrible. First of all, to
the Whites you are not Gorky the writer, but a Bolshevik. . . .
They might take you as a hostage. That would be terrible. It is
senseless for you to stay in Petrograd." Gorky answered immediately, "You are wrong to worry about me. No one will
touch me. I cannot and must not leave here. . . . I have no
right to abandon people who have worked with me and do not
have the protection bestowed on me by my reputation as a
writer and certain services rendered to the nation."

A few months later, a vigorous Soviet counteroffensive was
to relieve the city. But in the meantime Germany, defeated by
the Allies, had surrendered, the Treaty of Brest-Litovsk had
become null and void, and the antirevolutionary military
leaders could count on the support of France and Britain. The
young republic of the Soviets was more than ever in danger of
death, and now a supposedly socialist writer was expressing
indignation at the "Red terror" that the new leaders were
imposing on the country to purge it of its dubious elements.
"You hear and listen to the lamentations of a few hundred
intellectuals about their 'horrible' incarceration for a few
weeks," Lenin wrote to Gorky, "but you don't hear the voice
of the masses, of the millions of workers and peasants who are
threatened by Denikin, Kolchak, Rodzyanko,[4] by the conspir-
ators. . . ." And during a conversation in the Kremlin he put it
even more forcefully: "What else do you want? Is it possible
to be humane in this incredibly ferocious fight? Where is
there a place for sensitivity and magnanimity? Europe has put

us in a state of blockage, we're deprived of the help of the European proletariat that we were counting on, counterrevolution is attacking us like a bear, from all directions, and you don't think we have a right to struggle, to resist?" Lenin liked to compare a revolution to the labor of childbirth, when the woman, "tortured, torn, bloody, and crazed with pain, is only a half-dead piece of meat." He quoted Marx and Engels, who spoke of the "long labor pains" that accompanied the transition from capitalism to socialism. Gorky listened to him respectfully, but was only half convinced.

Among Lenin's close collaborators, the one most ill-disposed toward Gorky was undoubtedly Zinovyev, who went so far as to have Gorky's private correspondence monitored. Whenever Gorky intervened in favor of a prisoner, Zinovyev did his best to thwart his efforts. He had conceived a strong hatred of Gorky's new companion, Baroness Maria Budberg, née Zakarevskaya, whom he suspected of being a "foreign agent."

Gorky, who was about to turn fifty-two, had recently separated from Maria Andreyeva "on friendly terms" and begun an affair with Maria Budberg, known as Mara, a lively, intelligent, and astute woman who spoke fluent French, English, and German. After becoming the widow of a Russian diplomat at twenty-seven, she had begun living with a British diplomat. Arrested and jailed by the Bolsheviks, then released, she had tried to escape from Russia, but again the Cheka had seized her. Gorky obtained her release and took her into his apartment, first as his secretary, then as his "official" mistress.

Following her advice, he refrained more and more from political activity. In his speech on the occasion of Lenin's fiftieth birthday, in 1920, he was careful to say nothing about the nation's present difficulties, but praised the bright future being prepared for it by its brilliant, tireless leader: "I see the earth transformed into a precious stone by the work of a free human race. All men have become rational. Each has a feeling of responsibility for everything done by him and around him. Garden cities flourish everywhere, adorned with majestic edifices. . . ."

Pending the realization of this ambitious dream, the country was sinking into darkness, disorder, and destitution. In 1920, a terrible famine gripped Russia and, recognizing the failure of his attempt to establish a "war communism," Lenin proclaimed the New Economic Policy (NEP), more moderate than the old one. At the same time, in the hope of getting help from the Western capitalist countries, the Soviet government tried to move closer to the intellectuals who were still hostile to it. On the initiative of the powerful Kamenev, Gorky formed an All-Russia Famine Relief Committee. Reassured by the presence of that free-minded writer, a number of non-Bolshevik intellectuals joined the committee. To prove that, in the face of a national calamity, they placed the interests of the people above their own political preferences, they elected Kamenev himself as their chairman. At first the organization functioned smoothly: its members drew up a plan of action, made speeches, appealed to world public opinion. Gorky published a series of articles in the European and American press, urging that "the country of Tolstoy, Dostoyevsky, Pavlov, Mussorgsky, and Glinka," as he called it, be saved from famine. He already believed that a liberal springtime was about to take the place of the dictatorship. But the Cheka was intently watching that hotbed of charitable enthusiasm. Secret agents noted everything said by the committee members. Suddenly they were thrown into prison, sent to Siberia, or expelled from Russia. The only ones who escaped the purge were the Bolshevik leader Kamenev, chairman of the committee, and the untouchable Gorky. The Soviet authorities never repeated that attempt at collaboration with the intelligentsia on an equal footing.

The dismantling of that assembly of men of goodwill plunged Gorky into despair. There were those who accused him of having drawn sympathizers into the committee to point

them out to the Cheka. He angrily denied having done anything so comtemptible. When he saw Kamenev in the Kremlin, he said to him bluntly, "You've made me an *agent
provocateur.* That's never happened to me before!"

In November 1920, the British writer H. G. Wells was
welcomed to Petrograd with great pomp and ceremony. In
spite of the famine, the illustrious visitor was given a lavish
banquet, with sausages for hors d'oeuvres and chocolate bars
for dessert. Opposite him sat Gorky, grave but affable. The
writer Amphitheatrov, hostile to the Soviets, raised his glass
and said to Wells, "You see here, Mr. Wells, well-dressed
people in a pleasant place. That's a fraud. . . . If all of us here
took off our outer clothes, you would see, Mr. Wells, our dirty
underwear, which hasn't been washed in a long time and is
falling to pieces." Furious, Gorky stood up and said, "It
seems to me that lamentations are out of place here!" He then
declared, as though talking to himself, "The revolution is in-
vincible. It will transform people and the world."

Out of favor with the leaders of the party, and reviled by the
few liberals who had survived the successive purges, Gorky
found himself in an increasingly precarious situation. He
owed his continued freedom only to Lenin's benevolence. For
some time now, Lenin had been more optimistic about the
future of the Soviet regime. After spectacular successes on all
fronts, the White forces of Deniken, Yudenich, Kolchak, and
Wrangel, only partially backed by the Western powers and
without support in the countryside, were in retreat. The vise
was loosening. Wrangel was heading for Turkey with the rem-
nants of his troops. The Bolsheviks could again think of making contact with Europe. This would be a good time to send
Gorky there as an emissary for their cause. Not only would it
rid the country of a bothersome protester, it would also let the
young republic be represented abroad by a writer who, because of his prestige, would win the sympathy of the Western
nations. Furthermore, Gorky's health was deteriorating—exhausted by his multiple activities, he was suffering from

rheumatism, gout, heart trouble, and a worsening of his tuberculosis—and he could not expect to get the care he
needed in disorganized, starving Russia.

But in 1921, when Lenin advised him to leave the country
for his health as well as for political reasons, Gorky refused to
go. Lenin insisted by letter: "You're spitting blood and you
still haven't left! You're being both disloyal and shortsighted.
In Europe, in a good sanatorium, you can get treatment and,
at the same time, do three times as much work. . . . Leave, go
and have yourself taken care of." This time, Gorky decided to
accept the proposal that had come to him from on high. But
first he wanted to make sure that his faithful secretary, Baroness Maria Budberg—Mara—would be safe from Zinovyev's
persecution, so he asked that she also be given a passport and
an exit visa.

He left his country at the end of 1921, wondering, with a
mixture of sadness and curiosity, relief and bitterness, how
long this new exile was going to last. When he began the first
one, he had been fleeing from the rigors of the czarist regime;
now he was fleeing from the intrigues of his Bolshevik friends.
It was as if there were no place on earth where his passionate,
demanding soul could find rest. Would he ever be in agreement with any government in the world?

16

SECOND EXILE

Gorky was attracted to Italy, with its mild climate and happy-go-lucky inhabitants, but the Italian authorities refused to let a revolutionary writer, and personal friend of Lenin, enter their territory. His second choice was Germany, a country recently converted to democracy, bled white by the war, and well disposed toward Soviet Russia since the signing of the Treaty of Brest-Litovsk. He went to a sanatorium in the Black Forest. By Lenin's order, all his expenses were paid by the party. "Rest and take good care of yourself," Lenin wrote to him. "I am taking care of myself," he replied. "I spend two hours a day lying outside, no matter what the weather. They don't pamper the patients here: even if it's raining or snowing, stay lying down! And we stay lying down. There are two hundred and sixty-three of us here, each more tubercular than the next."

After that course of treatment he went to Berlin. The following summer he was at Heringsdorf, a fashionable beach on the Baltic shore. He stayed in a rather large house and, as in Russia, he was surrounded by a motley group of voluble guests. Nina Berberova, a Russian writer who visited him in July 1922, noted the emotion she felt at the sight of that tall, thin "old man" (he was fifty-four!) with tired blue eyes and a soft, hoarse voice. "He had," she said, "a rather condescending smile that did not always please everyone, and a face that could become unfriendly." She added, however, that in spite of his gruff appearance he had "the natural charm of a wise man who was like no one else and had lived a great, difficult, and extraordinary life." In conversation he freely criticized the intransigence of Bolshevik leaders, the harshness of Soviet censorship, and the disorder that reigned in the House of Writers, but in spite of his acrimonious words it was clear that he felt homesick for his country.

In the autumn of 1922, Gorky left Heringsdorf to spend the winter on the outskirts of Berlin, in a rented house across the street from a railroad station, near a small lake. He lived there with his son Max, his daughter-in-law (Max was now married), and Mara Budberg. On Sundays the house was full of visitors, often including Maria Andreyeva, red-haired, exuberant, heavily perfumed, toying with her rings and speaking with authority. But she stayed away whenever Gorky was visited by Ekaterina, who came straight from the Kremlin, "vibrant with political sensations."

There were often more than twenty people at table. Mara Budberg acted as the hostess. Vladimir Pozner, one of Gorky's visitors, described her as "a tall, solidly built young woman with sea green eyes, a dull complexion, and prominent cheekbones." "She was Gorky's secretary and friend," said Nina Berberova, "and while she was probably not the prettiest of all the women he had had, she was certainly the most intelligent." It was Mara who poured the soup into the plates, "always, for some reason, the same soup with dumplings." During the loud, rambling conversation, Gorky drummed his fingers on the edge of the table, which with him was a sign of ill humor. Then he would brusquely give his opinion. "It was impossible to argue with him," noted Nina Berberova. "Convincing him of anything was all the harder because he had an amazing ability not to hear anything that displeased him. He would turn a deaf ear to you so well that all you could do was stop talking. Or sometimes he would stand up, glaring, red-faced with anger, and walk toward his study, then stop in the doorway and say, by way of conclusion, 'No, that's not how it is!' And the discussion was over."

Young Vladimir Pozner was captivated by his almost childish gaiety, his propensity for improvising epigrams and puns, and the ease with which he went from fury to tears. Once when Pozner recited some poetry for him, Gorky suddenly began weeping. "That's how my eyes are made," he said apologetically. And he also said, "Happiness moves me to tears, but I feel unhappiness in silence."

In Berlin, hoping to reconcile Russian émigré writers and Soviet writers, Gorky founded a magazine, *Talk*, which published Blok, Sologub, Biely, and Remizov, among others. But in spite of his efforts, reconciliation proved to be impossible. There were too many differences between those who had left Russia to escape from the dictatorship of the proletariat and those who had chosen to stay in the country. The magazine appeared irregularly. After six issues it quietly expired.

The Russian émigrés were implacably hostile to that deserter from the "communist paradise" who had taken refuge in the "bourgeois hell." In Paris, Tatiana Alexinsky published a vengeful article, in French, in the June 7, 1922, issue of *Le Journal des Débats*, denouncing Gorky's "ill will and bad acts." "He has entered the top administration of those same Soviets that have established censorship of the press and shut down all non-Bolshevik newspapers and magazines," she wrote. "What post did he take among the Bolsheviks? The post of supreme corrupter of the intellectuals. He was appointed 'director of the literary section of state publications.' He had exclusive control of literary publishing and he became the distributor of subsidies to starving writers. Those who were willing to work with him could live, the others could only die of hunger. But unfortunately that was not all. Gorky proclaimed his sympathy with the Bolsheviks in cases where an elementary feeling of self-respect should have made him keep silent. When a young revolutionary, revolted by Bolshevik tyranny, tried to kill Lenin, Gorky prostrated himself before the dictator with a message of servile congratulations. When, in Petrograd, a young socialist student killed the bloodthirsty Uritsky (a former Okhrana agent who had become a communist policeman), the Bolsheviks took vengeance that same night by slaughtering fifteen hundred hostages and political prisoners in Petrograd prisons. After that monstrous crime, Gorky attended a meeting of the Petrograd Soviet among the members of its presidium, including the professional murderer Zinovyev; another Red murderer, Zorin, and other drinkers of Russian blood. . . . To us Russians, Gorky is one of those who are morally and politically responsible for the great calamities that the Bolshevik regime has brought to our country. Years will pass, but he will never be forgotten."

Gorky, of course, knew all about the terrible accusations made against him by his political enemies, among whom were many leftists. Some of them hoped that his stay abroad would turn him against the Soviet government. Surely he would regain his perspective when he contrasted the affluence, tolerance, and freedom of thought in western Europe with the oppression of the Bolshevik regime. But Gorky remained intractable. Though he was willing to criticize one of the Kremlin's projects now and then, on the whole he remained convinced that sooner or later the communist experiment would lead to a paradise of peace, brotherhood, and abundance. Even the methodical shooting of suspects, in the course of which the poet Nikolai Gumilev, notably, was killed, did not shake his faith. In July 1922, he sent the *Manchester Guardian* an article in which he admitted that he had been mistaken in condemning the Russian Revolution for its violence and disorder at its beginning; if Lenin and his group had not taken power at that time, he said, there would inevitably have been a horribly violent explosion of anarchy in Russia. And in September, to clarify his attitude toward the Soviet government, he published an outspoken article in the *Eve*, a Russian newspaper in Berlin: "A rumor is being circulated that my attitude toward the Soviet government has changed. I feel it necessary to state that, for me, Soviet political power is the only force capable of overcoming the inertia of the Russian masses, of rousing their energy and bringing them to create new forms of life, more just and rational forms; but my nature prevents me from siding with the attitude of Soviet political power toward the intelligentsia. I regard that attitude as a mistake. . . . Scientists and technicians are creators of new forms of life, as much so as Lenin, Trotsky, Krasin, Rykov, and the other leaders of the greatest of revolutions."

To show his attachment to the Soviet motherland, he gave lectures, drew up petitions, and organized collections of money for famine victims.

During the winter of 1923–24 Gorky stayed in Marienbad. Highly animated in summer, the town dozed in chilly isolation in winter. Only one form of entertainment: the cinema. Every Saturday there was a showing of *The Last Days of Pompeii*, *The Two Orphans*, or a Max Linder film. Since Gorky's visitors were less numerous at this time of year, he settled down to work on his new novel, *The Artamonov Business*. In it he depicted workers gaining political awareness in opposition to a bourgeois family of industrialists, the Artamonovs, and the slow disintegration of that clan beneath the blows of the forward-moving revolution. "Everything here comes from us!" say the workers. "We're the owners!"

At this time Gorky planned to go to southern France but his request for a visa was denied, despite the intercession of Anatole France, Romain Rolland, and Henri Barbusse. More accommodating, Mussolini's Italy opened its border to him in the spring of 1924. He was not allowed to stay in Capri, however, for fear that his presence there might stir up "certain political passions." He decided to stay on the mainland just opposite the enchanting island, at Sorrento.

Meanwhile, Gorky's situation with regard to the Soviet Union had become still more complicated. He bristled with anger at some decisions made by the Moscow government. There were times when the witless intolerance of the Bolshevik leaders made him feel that he had the sick soul of a liberal in the days of the czars. In 1923, he learned that the Soviet authorities had drawn up an "index" of forbidden books, which were to be immediately withdrawn from public libraries because of their antirevolutionary content. Some of the condemned authors were Plato, Kant, Schopenhauer, Ruskin, Nietzsche, Taine, Solovyov, Tolstoy, and Lesdov. Unable to swallow this pill, Gorky wrote to Khodasevich, "I can't believe that such spiritual vampirism really exists, and I won't believe it till I've seen the 'index' with my own eyes. But my first reaction was so strong that I began writing a letter to Moscow saying that I was renouncing my Soviet citizenship. What can I do if that bestiality proves to be true? If you only knew how painful my moral situation is!"

Though he did not renounce his Soviet citizenship—it would have mortally wounded him—he did briefly consider writing for a Russian émigré magazine that systematically attacked the Soviet regime. But the prudent Mara Budberg dissuaded him from taking that risky step. She herself was a monarchist by nature, but she felt that if Gorky broke with Moscow he would be making a double mistake: first, he would soon regret having betrayed the revolutionary ideal of his youth; and second, living abroad and being deprived of the subsidies paid to him from the party's treasury, he would find himself in a precarious financial position. It would be better to maintain his official ties to the government and reserve the right to lash out against it now and then.

While Mara Budberg's exhortations were inspired by prac-
tical considerations, Ekaterina Peshkov's sprang from zealous
revolutionary ideology. That "tiny and gracious" woman, to
use Gorky's description, had frequented people from the
Kremlin so much that she had become a faithful emissary of
the government. Intoxicated with high-level politics, she kept
close watch on Gorky's relations with the Soviet authorities.
Whenever he strayed from orthodoxy, she would write him a
letter urging him to get back in line. She kept him on a tight
leash and he accepted that constraint with angry gratitude.

In January 1924, when Gorky learned of Lenin's death, he
was overwhelmed with grief and anxiety. He had been expecting it because Lenin, having suffered a stroke, had for the
past two years been surviving only precariously and dealing
less and less with the details of running the country. But the
great leader had still been there, surrounded by respect, and
his words had been listened to. Despite their differences of
opinion, Gorky had known he could count on the friendly
support of Russia's guide. What was going to happen, now
that he no longer had a protector? When Ekaterina sent him a
telegram asking what inscription she should put on the wreath
that would be laid on Lenin's coffin, he answered, "Put on the
wreath: 'Farewell, my friend.'" On February 4 he wrote to
Maria Andreyeva, "I have received your very good letter
about Lenin. I have written my memories of him. . . . While I
wrote, I wept bitterly. I was not so unhappy even after Tolstoy's death. Now, as I am writing to you, my hand trembles."
The émigré press rejoiced over the death of Russia's "bloodthirsty master," and Gorky gave vent to his anger at this in a
letter to Ekaterina on February 11: "Till Lenin's death, in
spite of the ignominy and mediocrity of the émigré press I felt
pity, commiseration, etc., for the émigrés as a whole. Their
reaction to Lenin's death, a sickly, putrid reaction full of insane hatred, has completely cured me of those feelings. . . . I
had never before seen such a magnificent display of human

stupidity and viciousness. Those people treat themselves un-
mercifully by shamelessly revealing their rottenness. It is distressing to see how quickly unburied corpses decompose."

It suddenly seemed to him that with Lenin's death his exile
had taken a turn for the worse, that he had moved a little
farther from Russia. To maintain spiritual ties with his country, he invited the few Soviet writers who traveled abroad to
visit him in Sorrento. They were, of course, "reliable" people
on propaganda missions. One of them, Vsevolov Ivanov,
found him painfully homesick. When he enthusiastically
praised the climate of Italy and the gaiety of its inhabitants,
Gorky said to him, "In general, the Italians are an amusing
people. They're affectionately talkative and charming, and
they're always singing, but, as fascists, they're repulsive. It's
becoming harder and harder for me to live with them. . . . It's
agonizing to live here, and the climate of Italy is unpleasant
for me."

The powerful attraction he felt toward the Russian land and
the Russian people made him inclined to denigrate everything
foreign. Even the new Soviet literature seemed to him richer,
truer, and more useful than Western literature. "For a long
time I thought we were inferior to the Europeans in art," he
said to Ivanov. "But now I'm beginning to doubt it. The
French have produced Proust, who writes thirty-line, unpunc-
tuated sentences about trifles, and now it's hard to distinguish
Duhamel from Martin du Gard and Jules Romains from Mac
Orlan. They're all alike, and equally boring. In Italy, literature is absent. If you read English writers, you'll be struck by
their naiveté and their dependence on Dostoyevsky,
Nietzsche, and even Anatole France. There's nothing remarkable about the Germans, either." Yet he corresponded with
many first-rate European writers: Stefan Zweig, George Bernard Shaw, H. G. Wells, Franz Hellens, Thomas Mann, Knut
Hamsun, Anatole France, Henri Barbusse, Romain Rolland.
He had even accepted membership in the Pen Club, founded
by Galsworthy in 1921. His harsh judgment of everything

published outside of Russia was especially rash because, not knowing any language other than his own, he read foreign books in Russian translations that were often flawed. Among French writers, the only ones who found favor with him were Barbusse, because of his professed communism, and Romain Rolland, because of his love for the people and because during the war he had defied the insults of nationalists and bravely held himself "above the battle."

Without having met in person, Gorky and Rolland corresponded regularly in a spirit of warm friendship and mutual esteem. In their letters a great deal of space was devoted to political and cultural life, and socialist ideology, but sometimes they also spoke of their own writing. When Rolland praised *My Universities*, recently translated into French, Gorky replied on November 6, 1923, that he did not deserve such indulgence: "I know my faults well. The greatest one is excessive haste, being in a hurry to tell what I have seen, what I know, and what moves me. I am overloaded with real impressions, I am afflicted with an overdeveloped need to become acquainted with things, I am too easily fascinated by their external characteristics. That makes me more a storyteller than an investigator of the mystery of the human soul and the enigmas of life." And he defined his ideal as "to write like Flaubert." In his reply, Rolland defended Gorky's spontaneous art against the impersonal perfection of his French model. But Gorky stuck to his opinion.

And so the two men carried on heart-to-heart conversations from one country to another. Sometimes Gorky would hand Nina Berberova a thin sheet of paper covered with neat, elegant handwriting "reminiscent of Arabic manuscripts" and ask her to give him a Russian translation of that letter from his faraway friend Romain Rolland. In the evening he would bring her his answer and she would translate it into French. In difficult cases, several people would gather in his room for a collective translation. But while he was glad of his affectionate relations with Rolland, Gorky could not count on that refined utopian to familiarize him, the unpolished Russian Bolshevik sympathizer, with the art, morals, customs, and spirit of Europe.

To him, the Russian émigré writers were in a totally different category. Among those who had fled from Russia or been expelled, there were people of great talent and character: Bunin, Kuprin, Andreyev, Shmelev, Remizov, Zaitsev, Merezhkovsky, Artsybashev, Balmont, Zenaida Hippius, Aldanov. At first, Gorky had hoped to convert those misguided colleagues to his cause. But he had quickly realized that most of them were intransigent enemies of the new regime. They saw Gorky not as a sincere conciliator but as an ambassador of the devil. His very presence in the West, with his expenses paid by the Soviet government, seemed to them an insult to their misfortune. Bunin, who had been his admirer and friend, had abruptly turned against him. Earlier, in 1917, when Ekaterina had called him on the telephone in Moscow to tell him that Gorky wanted to talk to him, he had replied curtly, "We have nothing more to say to each other and I consider that our relations are permanently ended." When he became an émigré, he concentrated his anger against the writer who, to him, personified the barbaric madness and oppressive deceit of the Russian Revolution.

This animosity increased when, after the death of Dzerzhinsky, head of the Cheka, on July 20, 1926, Gorky gave in to pressure from Ekaterina and wrote an official letter deploring the loss of such a remarkable man: "I am absolutely overwhelmed by the death of Feliks Edmundovich [Dzerzhinsky]. I was rather closely acquainted with him in 1918–1921, and I had occasion to discuss delicate subjects with him. I importuned him about various matters and, because he was gifted with a sensitive heart and a strong sense of justice, we did a great deal of good." This message of condolence, made public by the Soviet press, stirred up a wave of indignation among the Russian émigrés, nearly all of whom had had at least one of their relatives imprisoned, sent to Siberia, or shot by order of Dzerzhinsky, the man "with a sensitive heart."

Detested for his opportunism by the majority of Russian writers living abroad, Gorky expressed his contempt for them in a letter to the Soviet writer Fedin: "I am amazed and almost horrified to see how men who only yesterday were 'cultivated' are now rotting in a loathsome way. Zaitsev writes mediocre books on the lives of the saints, Shmelev is so hysterical as to be unbearable, Kuprin drinks instead of writing, Bunin rewrites *The Kreutzer Sonata* under the title of *Mitya's Love*, Aldanov also copies Tolstoy. I will not even speak of Merezhkovsky and Hippius. You cannot imagine how hard it is to have to note all that."

That hatred between blood brothers, that continuation of the civil war beyond the national borders, strengthened Gorky's feeling that only Russia could bring him peace of soul. Yet he still could not make up his mind to return. He was too afraid of being disappointed by what he would see. "Abroad, you feel very ill at ease," he wrote in another letter to Fedin, "because everything is rotting slowly but surely, yet it is good to be there because you think intensely about all the great questions."

Gorky had no qualms about enjoying the material and intellectual comforts of the West while constantly proclaiming his country's superiority in all things. Tired and sick, he was preoccupied above all with finishing his life's work. He wrote up to twelve hours a day, leaning over his desk like a craftsman over his workbench and smoking one cigarette after another. "You must write every day at the same times," he said. "It soon becomes a habit." His handwriting was even, round, and painstaking. He wrote with a dip pen and refused to use a fountain pen. As for the typewriter, he regarded it as too modern, a machine that "broke the rhythm of the sentence." He was carefully dressed from early morning on. His clothes were always freshly ironed. He liked blue shirts, which harmonized with the color of his eyes, and he hated neckties. Mara Budberg and his son Max did his secretarial work. As in Capri, he received piles of letters and scrupulously answered them.

But most of his time was now devoted to writing a long novel, *The Life of Klim Samgin*. In it he depicted life in intellectually advanced circles in Russia before the 1917 revolutions. Klim Samgin, the main character, "an intellectual of average type," goes through the storms that shake his country and tries to see himself and the future clearly. This epic in several volumes was a sharp attack against liberals in the intelligentsia who, unable to break away from capitalism, had soon found themselves siding with the relentless enemies of the revolution. A few years later, referring to the didactic intentions of his novel in a debate with other Russian writers on June 12, 1931, Gorky said, "Emigré intellectuals living abroad spread slander about Soviet Russia, foment plots, and in general, behave basely; most of those intellectuals are Samgins."

The more he worked on his novel, the more his concept of it expanded. "I will still be writing it for a long time, more than a year," he told Fedin in a letter dated June 2, 1925. "It will be something enormous; not a novel, but a chronicle of the years from 1880 to 1918. I do not know if I can finish it. The theme is interesting: men who have invented themselves." And in December 1925, to Shishkov, "When will I come back to Russia? When will I finish the enormous novel I have begun? It will probably take me at least a year. In Russia, I will not work. I will travel all over the country, as you are doing."

So, to put off his return to Russia he gave himself the excuse of having a long novel to finish. This professional obligation put him at peace with his political conscience. Furthermore, he was sick and dreaded the fatigue of travel. "I have nothing good to say about my health," he wrote to Gruzdev on September 23, 1926. "My right arm is devilishly painful just below the shoulder and I have headaches, which I never had before. Add to that a case of bronchitis, a gift from autumn. It all bothers me terribly. I am writing the second volume of my novel and can do nothing else."

Meanwhile, more and more pressing letters were coming to him from Russia, begging him to return to his country, where he had become an idol of the masses. Workers, peasants, and intellectuals called out their love to him from far away. "All of Soviet Russia thinks of you constantly, wondering where you are and how your health is," the poet Yesenin wrote to him. "That health is very dear to us."

Ekaterina made a special trip to Sorrento to persuade him to end his "voluntary exile" and come back to Russia. She brought him the Kremlin's assurance that it was safe for him to return. To help persuade him, she called on their son Max, who was living in Sorrento with his wife, in pleasant idleness. Max, now nearing thirty, was a cheerful young man of rather limited intelligence, passionately interested in motorcycles and cars. His mother described the opulent life he would lead in Russia if he went back there with his father. Captivated, he urged Gorky to pack up and leave. The combined insistence of Max and his mother shook Gorky's determination to stay. But among those opposed to his leaving was Mara Budberg. Having bad memories of the time she had spent in Cheka prisons, she felt much safer abroad than in the Soviet Union. She persistently told Gorky that nowhere in Russia would he find the comfort and calm that he needed in order to continue his writing.

Torn between those who wanted him to go to Moscow and those who wanted him to stay in Sorrento, he was irritated by his own indecision in such an important matter. And his irritation was overlaid with uneasiness about the future of the Soviets. The articles in Western papers that Mara translated for him every morning made him wonder if the Bolshevik regime could hold out much longer against the disaffection of the peasants and the threat of economic disaster that hung over the nation. "You understand," he said, "they [the leaders of the Soviets] are only a handful of men, while there are millions and millions of peasants. . . . Some day the peasants will blow them away like a hurricane." And Vladimir Pozner noted, after a visit to Gorky, "He mistrusts the peasants and is afraid there may be a tidal wave that will sweep away the proletariat and the intellectuals."

Eventually, however, Gorky's homesickness became so great that it overrode all his fears. He could no longer bear the noisy demonstrations of Italian fascism. His émigré compatriots had become his worst enemies. Their animosity created around him a kind of emotional exile, which, added to his physical exile, drove him to depression. Everything foreign seemed odious to him. He desperately tried to convince himself that in Russia, despite the government's mistakes, a proud, hard-working, and educated humanity was being born. When one of his correspondents, Ekaterina Kuskova, asked him about his true feelings with regard to the Soviet regime, he answered haughtily in a letter dated August 19, 1925: "My relations with the Soviet Union are quite clear. I see no other possible regime for the Russian people, I think of no other, I want no other." And in an article titled *Ten Years*, published in 1927, he proclaimed his faith in the bright future of the U.S.S.R.: "The new Russian man, builder of a new state, is my joy and pride. To that small but immense man, who is found all over the country—in factories, in villages, on the remote steppes, in the forests of Siberia, in the mountains of the Caucasus, on the northern tundra—to that often lonely man, working among people who still cannot easily understand him, I address my heartfelt greetings. Comrade, I want you to know and be firmly convinced that you are the most necessary man on this earth. In doing your humble work, you have begun to create a new world." And *Pravda* published his tribute to Lenin: "His superhuman will has not disappeared; it remains on earth, embodied in the people. . . . The world was awaiting that man; he came, he showed the way, and people will follow that way indefinitely, seeing before them the radiant face of their immortal leader."

It was in this state of nationalistic, pro-Bolshevik exaltation that he finally decided to go back to his country. He dreaded the thought of what he was going to discover, and at the same time he felt an overpowering need to see Russian horizons, hear Russian voices, smell Russian odors. He prepared for the trip with feverish excitement and no one in his house dared to argue with him.

On March 25, 1928, on the occasion of his sixtieth birthday, the *New York Times* printed a congratulatory message followed by some fifty signatures. Enthusiastic telegrams from all over the world were sent to Soviet newspapers, which triumphantly displayed them in their pages. Some of the greatest Western writers—Romain Rolland, Stefan Zweig, Heinrich Mann, John Galsworthy, Georges Duhamel, H. G. Wells, Selma Lagerlöf—paid homage to the Russian revolutionary in Sorrento.

In the spring of 1928, having finished the second volume of *Klim Samgin*, he made his final preparations for departure. On May 20, he left Sorrento with his son Max and headed for Moscow. His second exile, like his first, had lasted nearly seven years.

17

THE OFFICIAL SPOKESMAN

The Russia to which Gorky was returning was no longer quite the same as the one he had left several years earlier. The regime had strengthened its grip on power by eliminating its main opponents. Stalin, the general secretary of the Central Committee of the Communist Party, had replaced Lenin as head of state. But, on the whole, the new leaders of the U.S.S.R. were very well disposed toward the writer who was coming back to the fold. They saw him as a man capable of uniting the workers and peasants in useful enthusiasm, a symbol of the humble people who had emerged from darkness and come into the light. After having served the regime abroad, he must now be able to serve it at home.

Gorky himself had an ardent desire to be convinced that the socialist experiment had succeeded. Having staked his whole life on that card, he could not accept the risk of being mistaken. After having so often criticized the distortion of the pure revolutionary idea by the comrades in charge of putting it into practice, he was determined that when he returned to his country he would approve and admire everything, out of love for the Russian land, technological progress, and the working masses. In his books he had forcefully denounced the people's flaws, but he now intended to celebrate their virtues. He felt he had to do it to give them confidence in themselves. His duty to the nation required him to embellish reality a little.

The press had unanimously announced his return as an outstandingly important event and an occasion for proletarian festivities. Joyous demonstrations began as soon as his train crossed the border from Poland. Crowds gathered at all stations along the way, holding up signs, bouquets of flowers, and streamers with words of welcome written on them. Choruses sang the *Internationale*. There were earnest, unaffected speeches. When Gorky got off the train in Moscow, he was greeted by a detachment of the Red Guard. The welcoming committee that came to meet him on the platform included political leaders, writers, and delegates from factories. How he was loved! How right he had been to come back! With compliments ringing in his ears and his heart aching with happiness, he expressed his gratitude again and again, in a choked voice. "I do not know if there has ever been a writer anywhere who was welcomed by his readers with so much friendship and jubilation," he said in an article he wrote for *Pravda*. "That jubilation dazed me. I am not presumptuous and I do not think that my work deserves such high appreciation. The most important and pleasant part of that encounter was what I saw and felt: young Soviet citizens know how to appraise and admire work. This means that they have realized and felt the deep significance—the international, worldwide significance—of the endeavor for which they are preparing themselves, and which they have already begun."

This declaration was exactly the kind of thing that the Soviet authorities expected of him. From then on he was caught up in a whirlwind of official receptions, visits to workers' clubs, conferences organized by unions, tours of factories, lectures in the House of Scholars. On one of those occasions he said, "It seems to me that I was away from Russia, not for six years, but for at least twenty. During that time, the country was rejuvenated. . . . I see before me a young country. And it seems to me that I myself have become young." He naturally paid a visit to the Lenin mausoleum. He stood there in meditative silence for half an hour. As he faced the embalmed corpse, he must have thought about the ideological quarrels that he had so often had with Lenin. Now the quarrels had ended with Gorky's happy submission.

So that he could better immerse himself in the nation, he sometimes wandered through the streets of Moscow in disguise, with a false beard, in search of new experiences. "It's the only way I can see without being immediately surrounded by a curious crowd," he wrote to Ekaterina on June 26, 1928. These anonymous contacts with the ordinary people of the city convinced him that literature had to be thoroughly renovated. At a meeting of writers he said, "Literature must be made more revolutionary than ever. How? I feel that it's essential to mix realism with romanticism."

From all directions, provincial cities begged Gorky to visit them. In July 1928, he responded, with the Kremlin's consent, by beginning a long journey across the country. He was accompanied by an escort of honor that the GPU (the secret police that had replaced the Cheka in 1922) had appointed. He was shown socialist farms, socialist schools, socialist factories, socialist penal colonies for delinquents. He described his impressions—always favorable—in the newspaper *Our Successes*, whose staff he had reorganized. Traveling tirelessly, he went south into Armenia and the Caucasus, came back toward Kazan, and stopped, his heart swelling with emotion, in Nizhni Novgorod. That city where he had been born and where he had lived as a beggar, despised by everyone, now welcomed him as the most illustrious of its sons.

Everywhere he went he gave speeches praising the regeneration of the people through awareness of their strength and genius. In Tiflis he said, "Comrades, today I have been called a happy man. It is true: you see before you a genuinely happy man, a man whose most beautiful dreams and hopes have been realized. The dreams may have been vague and the hopes indefinite, but they kept me alive and gave meaning to my life. If I were a critic and had to write about Gorky, I would say that the strength that made him what he is, as he is here before you, the writer you praise so exaggeratedly, the writer you love—that strength, I would say—comes from the fact that he was the first Russian writer, and perhaps simply the first person, to understand directly, by himself, the deep value of work, which organizes everything beautiful, great, and precious in this world." And in Nizhni Novgorod, in front of the municipal Soviet, he said, "In traveling over five thousand miles from Moscow to Yerevan and from Yerevan to Nizhni Novgorod, I received an enormous impression wherever I had to stop: the impression that in this country there is now an intelligent man who is his own master and is beginning to have an admirable understanding of his historical meaning." At a public meeting in Sormovo, an industrial town near Nizhni Novgorod, he praised the country's rulers: "I am not a party member, I am not a Communist, but I must tell you in all honesty that the party is truly your brain, your strength, your actual leader, a leader that the Western proletariat, to its great regret and misfortune, does not yet have."

These resounding declarations irritated Russian writers who had taken refuge abroad. One of them, Levinson, living in France, published in *Le Temps* an article accusing Gorky of having sold out to "the devil." This article was brought to Gorky's attention. He refused to respond to it publicly, but stated his opinion in a letter to the leftist magazine *Europe*, founded by Romain Rolland: "I am condemned for being on the side of the Bolsheviks, who reject freedom. Yes, I am on their side, because I am for the freedom of all honest workers and against the freedom of parasites and babblers. . . . I argued and quarreled with the Bolsheviks in 1918, when it seemed to me that they were not strong enough to dominate the peasants, who had been plunged into anarchy by the war, and that by clashing with that class they would ruin the workers' party. I later came to realize my mistake, and I am now absolutely sure that the Russian people, despite the animosity that all European governments have against them, and despite the serious economic difficulties that result from it, have entered the time of their resurrection."

Such benevolence toward the regime could not go unrewarded. When Gorky complained about great fatigue from his travels, he was allowed to go back to Sorrento to recover in a moderate climate. He left Moscow on October 12, 1928. In Sorrento, freed of his official obligations, he tried to regain his taste for writing. But again he felt obligated to devote his talents to glorifying the results achieved by the Soviet regime. In recounting his visits to Baku, Dnepropetrovsk, and Balakhna, he expressed uncritical wonder at nearly everything he described. "To speak of such factories," he wrote, referring to the paper mills in Balakhna, "one ought to write in verse, as though to celebrate the triumph of human reason." He urged his colleagues to avoid stressing the negative aspects of everyday life in Russia, and instead, to dedicate themselves body and soul to praising the victories of socialism. More than ever, he felt, utility took precedence over quality. Literature was conceivable only within the framework of propaganda. The times and the country required that attitude.

Ekaterina Kuskova, who had been expelled from the Soviet Union in 1921 after serving on the Famine Relief Committee, wrote to Gorky early in 1929 to reproach him for having a "one-sided" and therefore false view of Soviet reality. He answered her sharply: "You reproach me for my brutality toward the émigrés and my 'one-sided' view of Russian reality. . . . I will not speak of my brutality; it is probably in my nature. But in any case I do not consider myself more brutal than, for example, the aristocratic Bunin in his attitude toward people who do not think and feel as he does and, in general, toward the Russian masses. . . . A one-sided view? . . . But you yourself are one-sided—and greatly so!—in your letter. There is, however, one essential difference between us: you are used to not keeping quiet about things you find revolting. As for me, not only do I feel I have a right to keep quiet about them, but I even regard that ability as one of my best qualities. Immoral, you say? So be it. . . . The fact is that I have a sincere and implacable hatred of truth that is an abomination and a lie for 90 percent of the population. You probably know that while I was in Russia I publicly stated—in the press and at meetings of comrades—my opposition to 'self-criticism,' that habit of deafening and blinding people with the bad, harmful dust of everyday truth. I was unsuccessful, of course. But that does not dishearten me: I know that such truth is harmful to the 150 million human beings who make up the mass of the Russian people, and that all people need a different kind of truth, a truth that does not lessen, but heightens their energy in work and creation. This truth, which stimulates man's confidence in his will and reason, has already been sown in the masses and is giving excellent results. I do not care only about electrification, industrialization, the development of agriculture, and everything denigrated by your press. . . . What matters to me is the worker in a sugar refinery who reads Shelley in the original; what matters to me is the man who takes a broad, healthy interest in life, who realizes that he is building a new state; the man who does not live on words, but on his passion for work and activity. . . . You will say that I am an optimist, an idealist, a romantic, etc. Say it, that is your affair. Mine is to explain to you, as well as I can, why I am 'one-sided.' And, in that connection, remember that I began being 'one-sided' thirty-five years ago."

Gorky thus acknowledged that, to preserve the people's peace of mind and eagerness to work, they had to be kept from knowing the imperfections of the political system in which they lived. He pointed out all the errors of the old regime, but wanted to cover up those of the new one. The fiery anarchist of the past was now wearing rose-colored glasses. Out of love for his country, he preferred a sweetening lie to a bitter truth. He was not clearly aware of this transformation. He felt, in fact, that he had given up none of his youthful ideas, since he still placed the happiness of the proletariat above his personal concerns. Once again, in his eyes, the end justified the means. He even went so far as to say, "If the enemy does not surrender, he must be exterminated."

Gorky returned to Moscow at the end of May 1929, and he immediately resumed his activities as a journalist, a spokesman of the people, and an adviser of young Soviet writers. At the Fifth Congress of the Soviets he was elected to the executive committee. Soon afterward he attended the International Congress of Atheists as an appointed delegate and delivered a vehement speech. Meanwhile, he had founded a magazine, *Abroad.* But in June he went off on a fact-finding trip within the U.S.S.R., covering the northern regions and visiting the concentration camp on Solovetski Island in the White Sea, where common criminals and opponents of the regime shared the same appalling conditions. Even in that hell, he maintained his optimism. Since they had been convicted by the Soviet legal system, the people there could not fail to be aware of their crimes and glad of their punishment. After questioning a few prisoners he wrote, "Most of them give the clear impression that they have understood the main point— namely, that continuing to live as they lived before is impossible. After observing the behavior of the 'socially dangerous' elements, I must conclude that although the work of regeneration is painful for them, they realize that they must become 'socially useful.' This beneficial effect obviously results from the conditions in which those socially dangerous elements have been placed."

After this resolutely cheerful inspection he stopped in Leningrad, visited the museums, returned to Moscow, rested a few days in a house on the outskirts of the city and, on August 20, 1929, boarded the *Karl Liebknecht* and started down the Volga. During his long trip, which took him first to Astrakhan and Stalingrad, then to Rostov-on-Don and Tiflis, he made frequent stops to shake hands, kiss children, congratulate old workers, and shout slogans of the triumphant revolution to the crowds that gathered to see him. But between Tiflis and Vladikavkaz he began spitting blood and had to head back to Moscow. Rightly worried, he thought of Sorrento as the only place on earth where he could regain his vitality before plunging back into the fight.

Gorky went there in October 1929, and began recovering as best he could. He spent his time writing many articles, *Talks on the Trade*, *Memories of Lenin*, and a play, *Somov and Others*. His daily schedule was commendably regular. At nine in the morning he came into the dining room to have his breakfast with Mara Budberg, Max and his wife, and their two children: a cup of very strong coffee with milk and five lumps of sugar, a slice of bread without butter, and two raw eggs in a glass, mixed with lemon juice. Then he withdrew to his study and worked till two o'clock. After a frugal lunch, at which there were always guests, he walked along a path through pines and olive trees while his two granddaughters ran around him and diverted him with their shouts and laughter. Eventually he came to a bench and sat down on it, out of breath. Lighting a cigarette, he contemplated the landscape, the sea, Naples far off in the bluish haze, and Vesuvius.

Sometimes a friend went with him on his walk. In his memoirs, the writer Gladkov told how Gorky pointed to the horizon with his cane and said to him, "Admire that, engrave it in your memory. Here, nature is a carnival. Everything plays and sings: the sea, the mountains, the rocks. . . . But it's hard for me to get used to this festival of nature. Nature is transformed here into a false appearance, a theater set. . . . And the people lived wretchedly here. Gold and rags. Our country is stern in its beauty, but nearly everyone works hard there. The history of our people is the history of great work and a great struggle. An amazing people!"

After his breath of fresh air he came back to the house and worked in his study till dinner, which was served at eight o'clock. Then he played cards and talked. Max played his banjo, or else they listened to records. Gorky especially liked Grieg and Sibelius. Conversation with his guests, over tea, went on till late in the evening. The essayist Ilya Shkapa reported in his memoirs that once, when he questioned him about his firm commitment to Lenin after years of misunderstanding and criticism, Gorky said to him, "I'm not a politician. Only Lenin could see and understand everything. But he was a genius, a creator of events. . . . I was afraid that anarchy would make the revolution bog down in failure. . . . I'm not the only one who was mistaken. . . . Now everyone realizes that Lenin and his party were right at every stage of their fight. Peter the Great opened a window on Europe for Russia, and Lenin, in October, opened a window on the socialist future for all of humanity."

The fact that Gorky belonged to two eras—he began his career under czarism and brought it to complete fruition under socialism—made some writers see him as the "stormy petrel" he had celebrated in his poem. Carried away by his lyrical fervor, Aseyev wrote, "One of his wings plunges deeply into the shadows and silence of the time of the czars. . . . The other wing, raised high, lightened and cleansed of the dust of tradition and the weight of memory, soars freely at great altitude, illuminated by the light of a new era, by the young glow of dawn." And after scrutinizing Gorky, Aseyev noted, "His face expresses stubbornness and a refusal to agree with anyone in the world. But as soon as he is touched at a sensitive point, his face brightens." There was in him a mixture of obstinate brusqueness and naïve tenderness, of fury and kindness, of blindness and anxiety. One day, according to the Italian writer Aleramo, Tolstoy had said to Gorky, "It's strange that you're kind, when you would have had every right to be malicious. . . . Yes, you might be malicious. . . . But you're kind, and that's good."

Not everyone agreed with that. Among the émigrés, attacks against Gorky were more frequent than ever. In 1930, Bunin gave a lecture in Paris, at the Salle Gaveau, in which he denounced Gorky's duplicity, criticized his turgid style, and expressed surprise at his growing popularity. Gorky took no offense at these pinpricks, feeling that they were aimed less at him than at the Bolsheviks, whom he represented abroad. But he wrote to his biographer Gruzdev to point out some disturbing errors in the articles by Bunin that appeared in the Russian newspaper *Today.*

Even in Russia there were literary figures who condemned Gorky's determined efforts to use "Soviet humanism" to justify the worst trials and the most senseless executions. The poet Vladimir Mayakovsky had killed himself with a bullet in the heart on April 14, 1930, at the age of thirty-six, and it was said that his suicidal desperation was caused less by his unhappy romantic experiences than by governmental harassment. And Gorky was a friend of the functionaries in the Ministry of Culture. He himself had become a kind of literary functionary. He wore an invisible uniform that he seldom took off. "What was going on inside him?" Victor Serge later wrote. "We knew that he still grumbled, that he was uneasy, that his harshness had an obverse of protest and grief. We told each other: 'One of these days he'll explode!' And indeed he did, a short while before his death, finally breaking with Stalin. But all his collaborators on the *Novaya Zhizn (New Life)* of 1917 were disappearing into jail and he said nothing. Literature was dying and he said nothing. I happened to catch a glimpse of him in the street. Leaning back alone, in the rear seat of a big Lincoln car, he seemed remote from the street, remote from the life of Moscow, reduced to an algebraic cipher of himself. He had not aged, but rather thinned and dried, his head bony and cropped inside a Turkish skull-cap, his nose and cheekbones jutting, his eye-sockets hollow like a skeleton's. Here was an ascetic, emaciated figure, with nothing live in it except the will to exist and think. Could it, I wondered, be some kind of inner drying, stiffening and shrinking peculiar to old age, which had begun in him at the age of sixty?"[1] Gorky suffered not only from that "stiffening," but also from a kind of intellectual paralysis. The climate of Italy was beneficial to his painful joints and his confused mind. He rested, relaxed, and sometimes forgot the convulsions of his country in the throes of childbirth.

But an unexpected event broke the course of his calm, studious life in Sorrento. On the night of July 22, 1930 there was an earthquake. "It lasted forty-seven seconds in all," Gorky wrote to Gruzdev on July 27. "There was a terrible panic. Two o'clock in the morning. A stuffy night, an unusual silence. And suddenly the earth moved gently and groaned, trees shook, birds awoke, half-dressed peasants ran out of houses near ours, bells rang. . . ." And to Kryuchkov, on July 29, "The situation is horrible. Nearly a million homeless people. The poorest provinces were the hardest hit. Towns are totally destroyed, reduced to dust, and thousands of victims are buried under that dust." But Sorrento itself did not suffer greatly. When the alert had passed, Gorky's life resumed its routine of work, reading, and visitors. There was no question of moving away because of Vesuvius's whim. He did not really think of moving until the spring of 1931.

In May, Gorky was back in Moscow. There, as usual, he met with delegations of workers and pioneers, welcomed foreign intellectuals, including George Bernard Shaw, plowed through mountains of manuscripts, took an interest in the latest books published by his colleagues, submitted his play to wonder-struck actors, received a visit from Stalin and Voroshilov, and read them his old poem "The Maiden and Death." Stalin ostentatiously wrote on one page of that rather mediocre work, "This thing is greater than Goethe's *Faust*. Love, the conqueror of death. J. Stalin." And Voroshilov, not to be outdone, wrote on the next page, "For my part, I will say that I love Gorky as one of my own, as a writer from my own social class, a writer who, through his mind, has portrayed our forward march." Such flattering appreciations, from such lofty figures, could only encourage Gorky in his efforts to break new ground in literature. Not satisfied with writing himself, he also directed a series of publications: *History of Factories and Industrial Enterprises*, *History of the Civil War*, *History of the Young Man in the Nineteenth Century*, *Literary Apprenticeship*, *The U.S.S.R. Under Construction*. But his strength was fading. At the approach of winter, he again took refuge in Italy.

Vladimir Pozner, who saw him in Sorrento at about this time, noted that despite his nervous exhaustion he had changed little: "A few strands of silver shone in his hair and his moustache was still the color of light tobacco. There were two deep wrinkles in his cheeks. . . . His eyes were the same shade of blue and his voice had the same muffled sound." With Gorky were Mara Budberg, his son Max with his wife and their two little girls, a doctor, a nurse and several friends. Life in his pinkish yellow house surrounded by a flowering garden was exquisitely pleasant. He worked regularly, smoked all day long with his cigarette holder between his first two fingers, and held forth at great length during meals. His talk always came back to Russia. "I went to the Politburo, the Central Committee," he said, as reported by Pozner. "I just decided to go there. I saw ordinary workers who are statesmen. They know a lot and they're learning. Everyone is learning. Villages are migrating into the cities. The villagers don't want to live in the country anymore. They want cities to be built. And theaters. And cinemas." And, "What strength there is in our people! Before their strength was unused. Now it's being revealed. . . . They're a great people, not yet completely formed, not formed inwardly, anarchic. What's often not understood is that Lenin saved Russia from being devastated by the peasants. The countryside was marching against

the cities." And, "Everyone [in Russia] reads. The first printing of books are sold out in one day. If you go to the bookstore
the next day, it's too late!"

When warm weather returned in April 1932, he hurried
back to Russia and founded the series *Lives of Great Men* as
soon as he arrived. There was talk of his receiving the Nobel
Prize for literature. "We have again asked, within a limited
circle, that you finally be given the Nobel Prize," Stefan
Zweig wrote to him on May 10. "I hope your health is good
and that you are glad to be contemplating your country, which
we ourselves consider with growing hope. The stupidity of
Europe makes any sensible man ashamed. (As it turned out,
the British writer John Galsworthy received the Nobel Prize
that year.)

In August, Russian writers named Gorky to represent them
at the Pacifist Congress in Amsterdam, but the Dutch government refused to grant visas to the Soviet delegation. This was
not a complete surprise to Gorky. For some time he had been
stepping up his attacks on the West. With exacerbated pride,
he proclaimed the superiority of the Soviet Union over all
countries in the world, especially France, which was rotten,
and the United States, the land of the Almighty Dollar, gang-
sterism, racism, and lynching. Replying to an American journalist, he wrote, "I think that your civilization is the most
hideous on our planet because it has atrociously developed all
the shameful ugliness of European civilization." He even assailed, in *Izvestia*, Soviet writers and journalists who took the
liberty of jokingly criticizing their fellow citizens' way of life,
because in so doing they gave their country's adversaries a
pretext for denigrating the regime. In his anger, he compared
them with Noah's wretched son Ham, in the Bible, who inso-
lently neglected to cover his father's nakedness. "Our enemies imagine that they can 'put us in our place' with those
anecdotal truths," he wrote. "Let us leave them in the fog of
their illusions, but let us also see to it that the number of
scandalous anecdotes is reduced. . . . It is time for us to culti-

vate in ourselves the feeling of Pan-Soviet socialist responsibility and solidarity." In his opinion there were truths that should not be told, humor aimed at the regime was sacrilegious, and a dutiful Soviet writer should blindly praise the greatness of his motherland. In an article titled "Poetry" he went even further and exhorted his colleagues to turn away from the old, supposedly eternal themes—love, death, etc. —and develop new themes "belonging to the scientific sector of human activity." It was urgent that, in literature, debilitating analysis of mental states be replaced by celebration of industrial work.

What were the proportions of sincerity and opportunism in Gorky's devotion to the Soviet government? He was probably determined to convince himself that he was serving an ideal regime. His refusal to see its flaws came from his instinct of self-preservation. To stop believing in it would have meant renouncing his past, his integrity, his work, his life. It was better to lie to himself occasionally than to let excessive clear-headedness rob him of his reason for living. Those who took their desires for realities had the greatest chance of bending fate to their will. The future belonged to the fervent, not to the skeptical; to the zealous, not to the uncommitted; to people who wore blinders, not to those who looked left and right without making up their minds.

Gorky's repeated assurances of loyalty to the government brought him abundant honors. A committee was formed to celebrate his forty years of literary activity. A film was made about his life: *Our Gorky.* Theaters in Leningrad and Moscow presented his new play, *Yegor Bulychev and Others.* He was decorated with the Order of Lenin, the highest distinction that could be conferred on a civilian in the Soviet Union. In Moscow, an institute of literature was founded in his name. In Leningrad, he was again elected to membership in the academy from which he had been excluded twenty-five years earlier by order of the czar. And finally the supreme consecration: the city of Nizhni Novgorod gave up its name, which it had borne proudly for centuries, and became Gorky. One day its inhabitants woke up and found themselves "Gorkyans." Many other Soviet cities had been renamed to wipe away all traces of the czarist regime: Petrograd (the city of Peter the Great) had been Leningrad (the city of Lenin), Tsaritsyn (the city of the czar) had become Stalingrad (the city of Stalin), Yekaterinodar (the city of Catherine the Great) had become Krasnodar (the city of the Reds), and so on. But never before had a large city been named for a contemporary writer. Gorky had become a legend in his own lifetime. He belonged not only to literary history but also to geography. "Today, for the first time, I wrote 'Gorky' on an envelope instead of 'Nizhni Novgorod,'" he said. "It's embarrassing and a little unpleasant." He had the same reaction when he learned that the Soviet government had decided to add his name to the traditional name of the Moscow Art Theater. "Is it possible?" he asked, according to Valentin Khodasevich in his *Gorky As I Knew Him.* "Can anyone, if he wishes me well, give the name of Gorky to the Moscow Art Theater? And in front of all my compatriots! Ever since it was founded that theater had been Chekhov's! I don't know what to do!" While they were at it, the authorities renamed one of the great thoroughfares in Moscow: Tverskaya Street became Gorky Street.

To keep from drowning in that torrent of praise, Gorky told himself that, through him, it was the Russian people whom Stalin meant to glorify. The need to worship and believe had always been a trait of the Slavic race. The cult of personality was in the blood of that naïve and generous nation. In Gorky, who had come from its lowest level, it had found its intellectual model. Every line that came from his pen was declared proof of his genius. The newspapers tried to outdo each other in extravagantly eulogizing the author of *Mother.* It was as if admiring Gorky had become a civic duty in the Soviet Union. Never, in any other country in the world, had a living writer been the object of such adoration.

But he tried to keep a cool head. He must have found it

vaguely distressing to be acclaimed so fervently at a time when his creative powers had begun to abandon him. Would he not have better deserved that homage in his youth, when inspiration was seething in his veins? He felt angry despair as he continued working intermittently on *The Life of Klim Samgin*. What was that novel worth? What was his work worth, in general? He anxiously asked himself that question. In the Crimea, speaking of his books, Tolstoy had said to him, "You throw yourself at everything like a fighting cock. . . . Your language is very bold, even acrobatic; that won't do. You must write more simply. . . . Each of your stories has an assembly of reasoners, all expressing themselves in aphorisms. . . . You talk about yourself a great deal. . . . That's why there are no distinctive characters in your writing. Your characters are all alike. You probably don't understand women; you've never depicted one successfully."

Looking back on it, Gorky acknowledged that Tolstoy was right. His violent, abrupt, flamboyant style reflected the storminess of his anarchic temperament. He wrote as if he were taking vengeance, so that, he said, "the rich will feel a chill making their guts quiver." His intensity masked the poverty of his psychological analysis and the monotony of the subjects he wrote about so grandiloquently. While some of his youthful stories and his first novel, *Foma Gordeyev*, were full of vigorous life, the novels of his mature years, such as *Mother, Summer, The Little Town of Okurov, The Artamonov Business, The Three of Them*, and especially *Klim Samgin*, were ponderous and doctrinaire. He had to recognize that he was more at ease in autobiography. With its vitality and forthrightness, his autobiographical trilogy, *My Childhood, In the World*, and *My Universities*, seemed certain to be a lasting work, perhaps even an everlasting one. It laid bare the Russian people's basest instincts and most revolting coarseness. It spurted into the reader's face like an abscess full of pus. There was the same success for his play *The Lower Depths*, which, in its rags, remained strikingly current through time, translations, and performances. His other plays did not have that demonic robustness. They all had an air of militant political sermonizing about them. By trying to prove too much, a writer overshoots the mark and repels the public he hopes to win over. Even indignation becomes automatic and artificial. Gorky realized this, but could not resist his need to teach his compatriots. He believed in his mission as an educator, even if it should be a little detrimental to the artistic quality of his work.

When he thought of that work, he saw it as both revolutionary and traditional. He had inaugurated the era of Soviet literature, but he had his roots in czarist times. Whether he liked it or not, he was a living link between the great writers who had distinguished the last years of imperial Russia and the newcomers who adhered to socialist realism. With one foot in each of the two worlds, he, the self-taught man, ensured the continuity of Russian culture. He was both an innovator and a preserver, a pioneer who was nourished by the past.

He would have liked to devote all his remaining energy to writing a novel that would overshadow all his others. But he had to divide his time and energy among urgent activities that were useful to the nation. His most generous ambition was to shape the new proletarian literature. Feeling his strength declining, he was preoccupied with the question of who would take over when he was gone. As soon as a talented young writer appeared on the horizon, he was as glad as if it were a personal victory for him, and he worked to make the newcomer better known. Many beginners in the Soviet Union owed their success to him. To them, he was the father of writers, a magician from the dark depths of the nation, destined to guide everyone who felt the call to be a writer. His work as a journalist, publisher, propagandist, and literary adviser took up most of his time. He lived in a tumult incompatible with the demands of creation. He suffered from that tumult, yet he needed it as an excuse for the failure of his novelistic inspiration. By keeping busy, he could still give himself the illusion of producing.

In October 1932, he went to steep himself one last time in the soft light of Sorrento. But the calm of that refuge finally began to irritate him. It seemed to him that by going into exile for a few months he had placed himself outside the great movement animating the masses in the Soviet Union. He felt like a deserter at the thought that he was resting in that out-of-the-way part of fascist Italy while, far away from him, his own country was opening schools, building factories, and bringing electricity to the countryside. On May 9, 1933, he left Italy for good. On May 17, his ship landed at Odessa and he immediately took a train to Moscow.

Since coming to power, the Soviet government had seen to it that Gorky lived comfortably. After all, he was the official bard of the regime, a kind of "Minister of Creative Intelligence." He was spared all financial worries. When he returned to the Soviet Union he was given a luxurious three-story house with an art nouveau facade at 6 Malaya Nikitskaya Street, in the center of Moscow. Before the revolution it had belonged to the millionaire Ryabushinsky, a patron of symbolist and decadent poets. Gorky did not feel at ease in that huge building with overelaborate decoration. He preferred the other house he had been given, on a hill just outside Moscow. Thanks to the authorities' solicitude, he had at his disposal a car, a private secretary, and a doctor.

He had a large entourage and, like all prominent people, he was kept under close watch. Most of the many letters he received were full of extravagant praise, but occasionally there were anonymous ones condemning him for collaborating with the dictatorship. Some of them even threatened him. Now and then he received an envelope containing a piece of string tied in a hangman's noose. All this was enough to make the GPU enclose him in a net of spying and protection. That formidable organization, specializing in tracking down anti-revolutionaries, made arrests on the basis of unsupported accusations and judged its prisoners in quick secret proceedings. Even the highest officials feared its investigations. It was headed by Genrikh Yagoda, a coarse, unscrupulous man who had become Gorky's friend and supplied him with his secretary, Kryuchkov, and his doctor, Levin, both agents in his pay. He often visited Gorky and his family. And Gorky never thought of reproaching him for the thousands of victims who had died by his order, supposedly because they were enemies of the people.

Gorky lived on the second floor of the house on Malaya Nikitskaya Street. On the third floor were his son Max, his daughter-in-law Nadezhda, and his two granddaughters, Marfa and Daria. A trustworthy woman named Olympiada Chertkova had the responsibility of watching over his health and running his household. Beside his bright, spacious study was a room where his secretary opened the mail and answered the telephone. Kryuchkov also had the duty of shepherding the many visitors and making them wait till Gorky was ready to see them.

In the morning, Gorky worked on his novel or a short story; after lunch, he wrote articles and read and answered letters; after dinner, he received people who had favors to ask of him and, when the last of them had left, he read far into the night. He owned nearly ten thousand books, some of them with marginal notes in his hand. He also liked to accumulate "strange" objects: he was very proud of his collection of Japanese and Chinese bone statuettes. He liked classical music, hated jazz, and sometimes invited singers to come and sing Russian folk songs to him.

There were nearly always guests at his table. Writers, painters, actors, scholars, and politicians often gathered in the dining room, whose bay window overlooked the garden. It was, according to the writer Lev Nikulin, "a cultural center," a meeting place for the elite of the nation, "a beacon of thought and knowledge." "He was there," Vladimir Pozner wrote in his *Memories of Gorky,* "with his hands in his pockets, his shoulders rounded and his head, too small for his body, tilted a little to one side." As soon as he opened his mouth, everyone fell silent. Despite his sickness and his age, there was still youthful ardor in him. His eyes shone when, in his hoarse voice, he proclaimed his faith in the future of the Russian people. "If the human race woke up one day and found the earth transformed into a paradise," Pozner once heard him say, "do you think they'd be glad of it? Of course not! Do you know what they'd say? 'Who dared to make a paradise here while we were asleep? We don't want it. Paradise is something we'll make for ourselves!'"

He tirelessly developed that idea in his articles and speeches. And in discussions with his colleagues he firmly maintained the need to regulate the Russian language. "It's essential," he said, "that we work relentlessly to cleanse literature of verbal debris, and fight for the purity and clarity of our language, for an honest writing technique in which there is no specific ideology." *Pravda* and the government supported him in that campaign.

He also readily gave his opinion about the duties of the artist in the Soviet Union. On July 14, 1933, visiting an exhibition of paintings, he said to the journalists there, "Our painters must not be afraid of a certain idealization of Soviet reality and the new man. . . . As for the subjects of their paintings, I'd like to see more children's faces, more smiles, more spontaneous joy." That same day, in speaking to some Soviet sculptors, he said, "The artist deserves praise when he seeks new subjects and new plastic forms, but the result of his efforts must always be understandable to the people." A few years earlier, when a worker named Sapelov had asked him if a writer should give preference to the good or the bad side of life in his books, Gorky answered in a letter dated December 11, 1927: "I am in favor of emphasizing the good side. . . . The bad side is no worse than it always was, and the good side, in our country, is better than it has ever been, here or anywhere else." Later, in an article published by *Pravda* on March 9, 1935, he declared with the extravagance of patriotic pride, "Our literature is the most influential in the world."

Meanwhile, his main concern, the one that cost him the most time and energy, was making preparations for the first Congress of Soviet Writers. He wanted that international meeting to give the whole world proof of the power and variety of Russian genius under the new regime.

On August 17, 1934, six hundred delegates from fifty different nations chose Gorky as chairman of the assembly. He gave an opening speech in which he said, "Nowhere else in the world has there ever been a state where literature and science benefit from such fraternal aid as in the Soviet Union." All through the sixteen days the congress lasted, Gorky valiantly performed his duties as chairman, listening to all the speeches, talking with his colleagues between sessions, inviting them to visit him in his house on Malaya Nikitskaya Street. In the name of "revolutionary romanticism," the delegates, led by Gorky, condemned the works of Joyce, Proust, and Pirandello. The catch phrase was "Raise man above himself without detaching him from reality." The final resolution of the congress, adopted unanimously, stressed "the outstanding part played by the great proletarian writer Maxim Gorky" in the development of his nation's literary genius. He was elected president of the Union of Soviet Writers.

But this new honor could not cure him of a deep sorrow: three months earlier he had lost his son Max, an amiable, scatterbrained young man passionately interested in stamp collecting and car racing. Max had served as his father's interpreter and sometimes typed his manuscripts, and he had done some hard drinking with Dr. Levin and Kryuchkov, the secretary. When he fell ill, the doctors called to his bedside gave a diagnosis of pneumonia. Their treatment was ineffective. Max died on May 11, 1934.

The highest officials of the party and the government called on the grieving family. *Pravda* published many messages of condolence. Genrikh Yagoda, head of the GPU, acted as a faithful friend by coming every day to console Max's father and widow. But Gorky felt that with the death of his son— whom he had sometimes called a "likable nonentity" even though he loved him tenderly—the roots of his own life had been shaken. Only hard work could save him from despair.

He feverishly turned out one article after another, including "Talks With Youth" and "Proletarian Humanism." He even founded another magazine, the *Collective Farmer*. In December 1934, he was elected to the Moscow Soviet as a writers' delegate. One last bauble, one more obligation. He was no longer a man but an institution. Despite his infinite sadness, his fatigue, and his doubts, he was still standing, kept on his feet by the constraints of the official functions he had accepted out of conviction, a sense of duty, and sheer habit.

18

THE FINAL COMMITMENT

In spite of his repeatedly expressed desire to be the official praiser of the regime, Gorky could not be unaware of the dictatorial character that Stalin had given it. He knew that the country was living in constant terror; that no one dared to stand up to the authorities; that a ferocious purge was already extending to the traditional leaders of the party, including Trotsky, Zinovyev, and Kamenev. The new master of Russia was eliminating the old stalwarts one by one, on the pretext of all sorts of accusations. Those high-level settlings of scores worried Gorky, but he quickly reassured himself with the thought that concentrating power in one man's hands was probably necessary for the regeneration of a country that was by nature apathetic and disorderly. That utopian, once passionately devoted to freedom, was not troubled by all-out nationalization, police surveillance, denunciations for sordid motives, or the regimentation of thought in accordance with orders from above. Any form of constraint seemed good to him, as long as it had the excuse of being intended for the happiness of the proletariat. And that happiness, he was convinced, would soon be a reality.

He was thrown into consternation when Sergey Kirov, one of Stalin's chief aides, was assassinated on December 1, 1934. "I am absolutely overwhelmed by Kirov's murder," he wrote to Fedin. "I feel as if I had been broken into a thousand pieces. . . . I liked him and respected him as a man."

Kirov's death reopened the era of spectacular purges. There was talk of a vast conspiracy against the regime. Tried behind closed doors, the defendants acknowledged their errors, according to custom. Once again Stalin seized a chance to "liquidate" people he still mistrusted. And Gorky joined with the press in expressing approval.

Yet he did not have for Stalin the same affectionate admiration he had for Lenin. In his speeches and writings he celebrated Lenin's "genius," but with Stalin he simply spoke of a "will of iron." To him, Lenin was the creator of a new society and Stalin was a rigorous administrator. This distinction did not prevent him from appreciating the tokens of esteem that were lavished on him by the now uncontested ruler of the Soviet Union. A few kind words from Stalin about his books were enough to revitalize him for a time. In such cases he sometimes responded with an outpouring of enthusiasm. "Long live Stalin, the man with an immense heart and mind!" he exclaimed in July 1935.

Stalin visited him in his large house on the outskirts of Moscow. Gorky also received many Soviet writers there, and even some foreign writers, such as H. G. Wells and Henri Barbusse. In the summer of 1935, Romain Rolland and his wife came from France and spent several weeks with Gorky. Through an interpreter, the two men had animated conversations on politics and literature. During Rolland's visit, Gorky invited Stalin, Voroshilov, and other members of the government to his table, and had many films shown, including Eisenstein's *The Battleship Potemkin* and Pudovkin's *Mother*.

Rolland's brief stay was long enough for him to analyze the cause of Gorky's torment: he was torn between his desire for independence and his fascination with the new Russia, that "Pharaonic Russia" where "the peoples sing as they build their pyramids." "He was intoxicated by the whirlwind of multitudinous life in which he was caught," wrote Rolland, "and the individualist plunged into it. It was almost as if he found relief in moving away from the painful independence of his whole life and enrolling in the great army of the community. He professed his faith and did not argue; he is the foreman of a construction site: he supervises it and rouses or upbraids the workers." "But," added Rolland, "he does not deceive me: his weary smile tells me that the old anarchist is not dead. He still misses his vagabond life. . . . He is a weak man, very weak, actually, in spite of his bearish appearance and his violent outbursts. He is kind and affectionate; he is exposed."

Elsewhere, Rolland deplored the fact that Gorky was kept under surveillance by his secretary, Kryuchkov, a liaison agent of the government and the party. Kryuchkov, he noted in his *Journal du Voyage en U.R.S.S.*, "has placed himself in total control of communication with the outside: letters or visits (or rather, requests for visits), he intercepts everything; he alone is the judge of who will or will not reach Gorky." And finally this comment: "He is very lonely, though he is almost never alone! It seems to me that if we could have been together (and if the language barrier could have been broken), he might have hugged me and sobbed for a long time, without speaking."

Thus even a leftist full of admiration and affection for Gorky was struck by his emotional isolation amid the coming and going of visitors. He sensed Gorky's distress at being reduced to helplessness by his total submission to an ideology. In that champion of the people he saw primarily a prisoner. Muzzled by his entourage and his secretary, the "old bear," according to Rolland, had "a ring in his nose."

When Gorky and Rolland parted in July 1935, on a railroad platform in Moscow, they were two close friends who understood each other beyond words. Rolland took with him in his heart the memory of a sad, confused, and lonely man weighed down with his own glory.

Sometimes when he looked back over his past, Gorky had to acknowledge that he had followed a strange course: starting with freedom and a rejection of honors, he had ended with obedience and official consecration. Had he taken a wrong turn along the way? Had he ruined his life by making it too successful?

The truth is that ever since his reconciliation with the Bolsheviks, Gorky had been manipulated by the government. He sometimes realized that obvious fact but quickly rejected it with horror. The government had made use of his international prestige to beg for food from foreign countries in 1920, to try to make the intellectuals assent to the revolution in 1928, and to mobilize writers as "engineers of human souls" from 1932 on. All his years of maturity and old age had been taken away from pure art and placed in the service of political efficacy. In his enormous naïveté, he had become a pawn on the chessboard of the state. And it was inevitable. What other writer in the Soviet Union had his stature, his reputation in the eyes of the West? Most of the great contemporary Russian writers had chosen exile. For the Soviet authorities, Gorky was the only one who could usefully play the part of a paragon of revolutionary virtue, both at home and abroad.

On August 11, 1935, he went to the city that now bore his name, Gorky, and, with his daughter-in-law and two granddaughters, boarded a brand-new ship to go down the Volga. And it happened that this ship was named the *Maxim Gorky*. The trip was hard on him. Damp heat weighed down on the river. The vibration of the engines unsettled his nerves. He slept badly and breathed with difficulty. At each stop, however, he met delegations of workers and members of the local Soviets, and in speaking to them he tirelessly praised the cultural and industrial achievements he had seen.

A long rest in the Crimea failed to restore his health. There, too, he had many visitors, including André Malraux. Despite his illness he passionately talked with them about the talent of Aragon and Sholokhov. He was asked to attend the Congress for the Defense of Culture in Paris, but he was too weak to go. The house where he stayed in the Crimea was surrounded by a large abandoned park. He worked in it between writing sessions, spading lawns, clearing paths, planting flowers. Whenever he made any physical effort, he had a container of oxygen close at hand, and he used it at the slightest feeling of faintness. "I am afraid of only one thing," he wrote on March 22, 1936: "that my heart will stop before I have finished my novel."

On May 26, he decided to go back to Moscow. On the train, his car was swelteringly hot. Now and then a window had to be opened to freshen the air. Gorky panted, his lungs congested. Several times he inhaled oxygen for relief. He hoped for cool weather in Moscow, but it proved to be sultry, with a torrid wind blowing through the streets. He took refuge in his country house.

As soon as he arrived, he came down with a severe case of influenza. The bad state of his lungs and heart made this disquieting. Doctors Levin and Pletnev alternated in taking care of him, but could not bring his illness under control. On June 6, all the newspapers published reports on his health. But to avoid alarming him, a special issue of *Pravda*, in which there was no mention of his illness, was printed for him alone. Thousands of letters came into Kryuchkov's hands, all expressing the same wish: that the great writer, who had become the nation's spiritual father, would make a speedy recovery. Since he could not breathe lying down, he spent his days and nights in an armchair.

When he felt death approaching, his main regret was that

he had not been able to finish his novel *The Life of Klim Samgin*. But sometimes he felt a resurgence of his craving for action and struggle. "To live, just to live!" he said. "Each new day brings a miracle. And the future is so extraordinary that no imagination can foresee it!... We die too soon, much too soon!"

He summoned up his last remaining strength and, writing in pencil on little slips of paper, noted how he felt in his illness. "Things are getting heavier: books, pencils, the glass; and everything seems smaller than before." And, thinking of *Klim Samgin*, "End of the novel, end of the hero, end of the author." On June 16, he had an unexpected remission, shook hands with his doctors, and said to them, "I think I'm going to pull through."

But it was only a short respite. His fever returned and he began spitting blood. In his delirium he spoke in a faltering voice about the danger of a world conflagration: "There will be wars.... We must prepare...." On Sunday, June 18, 1936, he completely lost consciousness. At ten past eleven in the morning, Gorky died. Notified by telephone, the painter Korin came to make a death sketch of Gorky. He found him lying on his bed, wearing a light-blue blouse, "very thin and looking younger." Behind Korin, a molder waited for him to finish drawing so that he could make a death mask of Maxim Gorky.

In the name of the government and the party, the press and the radio immediately announced "the death of the great Russian writer, the brilliant artist of the word, devoted friend of the workers, fighter for the victory of communism." Stalin ordered a state funeral. Gorky's body lay in the Hall of Columns, attended by a guard of honor that included the highest dignitaries of the state: Stalin, Khrushchev, Mikoyan. Thousands of mourners came to pay their last respects. Then the body was cremated.

On June 20, there was a solemn farewell ceremony in Red Square. Stalin led the mourning, wearing a black armband.

Artillery thundered, orchestras played the *Internationale*, troops marched past. The urn containing the beloved writer's ashes was placed in a niche in the Kremlin wall, behind the Lenin mausoleum. It joined urns containing the ashes of all the great pioneers of the revolution. There were many speeches. In paying tribute to his illustrious colleague, the writer Alexey Tolstoy (a distant relative of Leo Tolstoy) said, "A great man's passage in history is not marked by two dates —that of his birth and that of his death—but by only one: the date of his birth." Having come to Moscow expressly to attend the funeral, André Gide also spoke in Red Square that day, as reported in his *Retour de l'U.R.S.S.*: "Comrades, Maxim Gorky's death darkens not only Russia but the whole world. The fate of culture is linked in our minds with the destiny of the Soviet Union. Maxim Gorky lent his voice to those who had not yet been able to make themselves heard. . . . Maxim Gorky now belongs to history. He takes his place among the greatest."

Gorky's death had overwhelmed the whole Russian people. Despite the efforts of propaganda, it was not his political speeches and articles that remained in their memory, but the harsh, deeply moving pages of *My Childhood, In the World,* and *My Universities,* and his lively portraits of such great writers as Tolstoy, Chekhov, Korolenko, and Andreyev.

Unlike some writers who suffer a drop in popularity immediately after their death, Gorky underwent no decline in his countrymen's admiration. Idolized during his lifetime, he was now idolized still more. But suddenly rumors alerted public opinion. Maybe there was something suspicious about Gorky's death. Had he been murdered by enemies of the regime? Even more troubling than the rumors was the startling arrest of Yagoda, who had been dismissed as head of the political police.

Finally, on March 3, 1938, more than twenty months after Gorky's death, the official Soviet press announced that the Supreme Court was going to try several prominent figures for high treason, secret communication with foreign countries, sabotage, conspiracy against national security, and terrorist acts. Among the victims of those terrorist acts were Maxim Gorky and his son Max, "medically assassinated" by order of Yagoda, head of the GPU, and "a bloc of rightists and Trotskyites." Also on trial, besides Yagoda and his sinister agents, were Rykov, one of Lenin's closest friends; Rakovsky and Krestinsky, former Soviet ambassadors; and Bukharin, the eminent Bolshevik theoretician who drew up the party's program.

This was the third great trial of its kind. As in the others, the exiled Trotsky was attacked through his "henchmen." According to the indictment, "the Judas Trotsky," "the main spy leader," had once again fomented a plot against some of the best servants of the regime. Since Gorky was a steadfast friend of Stalin, Trotsky had demanded that he be killed. The execution of that crime, under Yagoda's supervision, had been entrusted to Gorky's secretary Kryuchkov, who was to find a way to make him catch a cold or some other illness, and to Doctors Levin and Pletnev, who would hasten their patient's death instead of curing him. There was the "liquidation" procedure for the cheerful and harmless Max.

As was customary in such cases under Stalin's reign, the defendants "spontaneously" admitted their guilt. Under questioning by Vyshinsky, the state prosecutor, they even elaborated in morbid detail on the baseness of their intentions. They showed no sign of being troubled by the absurdity of the acts attributed to them. With their will broken, they recited lessons they had learned by heart in their cells. It was the two doctors who confessed their sins most forcefully. Yes, they had seen to it that Gorky caught a cold while working in his garden in the Crimea; yes, they had given him treatment designed to be harmful; yes, they had known they were committing a political and antirevolutionary murder. . . .

In his summation, Vyshinsky called the defendants "stinking piles of human garbage" and concluded by saying, "Our

whole country, from its little children to its old people, ex-
pects and asks only one thing: that the traitors and spies who
betrayed their country to the enemy be shot like abject
dogs. . . . Time will pass. The detestable traitors' graves will
be covered with weeds. . . . And above us, above our happy
country, the rays of our sun will shine joyfully. We will walk,
as before, along a path cleansed of the debauchery and filth of
the past, behind our beloved leader, the great Stalin. Forward, forward toward communism!"

The ten-day trial had a savage outcome: eighteen defendants, including Bukharin, Rykov, Yagoda, Krestinsky, Dr.
Levin, and Kryuchkov, were condemned to be shot, and their
executions took place without delay; three, including Dr.
Pletnev, were given long prison sentences.

Dr. Pletnev was sent to a concentration camp to serve his
twenty-five–year sentence. In 1948, he told Brigitta Gerland,
a prisoner who had become his assistant in the infirmary of
the camp, that Gorky was killed by order of Stalin. When
Gerland regained her freedom, she published Pletnev's story,
according to which Gorky, horrified by the climate of terror
that Stalin had imposed on the Soviet Union, wanted to go
back to Italy and threatened to make a public denunciation of
the regime. To prevent him from carrying out that threat, Stalin sent him a box of tasty-looking candy. Gorky gave some of
it to two nurses in his entourage and ate some of it himself.
The result came swiftly: horribly painful death. Autopsies ordered by Dr. Pletnev established the presence of poison in the
three bodies. "We doctors kept quiet," he said to Brigitta
Gerland, as reported by Yuri Annenkov in his *Diary of My
Encounters.* "Even when the Kremlin published a totally false
official version of Gorky's death, we didn't protest. But our
silence didn't save us. Rumors were spreading in Moscow;
everyone was whispering that Gorky had been murdered, poisoned by Stalin. Stalin had to divert the people's attention,
turn their suspicions in another direction, find other culprits.
The simplest solution, of course, was to accuse us doctors of

the crime. We were thrown into prison. . . . But why should we have poisoned Gorky? A stupid question—we were obviously acting under orders from the fascists and the capitalist monopolies!"

In pointing to Stalin as the only one responsible for Gorky's death, Pletnev was siding with Trotsky and everyone else who saw the master of the Kremlin not as a vigilant leader but as a bloodthirsty dictator. No one in the Soviet Union, of course, dared to repeat that accusation, even among intimate friends, for fear of immediate arrest.

The fact is that whether Stalin ordered Gorky's murder and attributed it to others, or disguised a natural death as a political crime, he scored a propaganda victory with the masses. As time passed, however, obfuscation among the public gave way to sensible skepticism. Despite the claims of the official press, many shrewd people, even in the Soviet Union, regarded the Stalinist assertion of Gorky's "medical assassination" as implausible. Sixty-eight years old, tubercular, exhausted, Gorky might very well have died of pneumonia without any criminal intervention. By staging the grotesque and tragic trial of the "bloc of rightists and Trotskyites," Stalin had tried to finish eliminating those whose popularity in the party appeared dangerous to his personal ascendancy. The death of the greatest Soviet writer had seemed to him an excellent pretext for giving the conflict a dramatic turn. There could be no better way of electrifying the masses than referring to an illustrious corpse.

And so, even after his death, the naïve, intransigent, and loyal Gorky continued to serve the regime.

NOTES

CHAPTER 1 HUMBLE ORIGINS

1. March 28, by the Gregorian calendar used in the rest of Europe. In the nineteenth century there was a twelve-day difference between it and the Julian calendar used in Russia.

2. All quotations in this chapter are from Gorky's *My Childhood*.

CHAPTER 2 THE VOLGA

1. All quotations in this chapter are from Gorky's *In the World*.

CHAPTER 3 YEARS OF APPRENTICESHIP

1. In this chapter, all quotations except the last one are from Gorky's *In the World*.

2. From Gorky's *My Universities*.

| CHAPTER 4 **STUDENTS**

1. In this chapter, all quotations except the last one are from Gorky's *My Universities.*

CHAPTER 5 **PEASANTS**

1. Russian journalist and philosopher (1842–1904).

CHAPTER 6 **FIRST LOVE**

1. From Gorky's *My Universities.*

CHAPTER 7 **MAXIM GORKY**

1. Gorky wrote about this long walk in his story "My Fellow Traveler."

CHAPTER 11 **BLOODY SUNDAY**

1. The Mordvins were a people who lived in the middle Volga basin and spoke a Finnic language.

CHAPTER 12 **THE EXILE'S RAGE**

1. October 13, 1907, by the Gregorian calendar. The difference between the Gregorian calendar and the Julian calendar used in Russia went from twelve days in the nineteenth century to thirteen in the twentieth.

CHAPTER 13 **CAPRI**

1. Zinovy Peshkov was born in Nizhni Novgorod in 1884. He was the older brother of Yakov Sverdlov, born in 1885, who was an active revolutionary and, beginning in 1917, the organizer of Bolshevik power and the Bolshevik Party. Yakov Sverdlov died in 1919. The city of Sverdlovsk, in the Urals, formerly Ekaterinberg, was named for him.

CHAPTER 14 **RETURN TO THE MOTHERLAND**

1. Zinovy Pechkov (the French spelling of Peshkov) continued his career brilliantly in France. A close collaborator of the Resident General in Morocco, in 1926 he was detached to the Ministry of Foreign Affairs. He was then placed in the service of the high

commissioner of the Levant (1930–39), and finally he was transferred to the government of South Lebanon. In 1941 he joined the Free French Forces. From 1941 to 1943 he held important posts in Africa. In 1944 he was promoted to brigadier general, appointed to the French Committee of National Liberation at Chungking, and given the position of French ambassador. In 1946 he headed the French liaison mission to General MacArthur in Tokyo. That same year he received the rank of lieutenant general and the title of Grand Officer of the Legion of Honor. He retired in 1949 and died in 1970.

2. Karl Kautsky (1854–1938), a German socialist.

3. Rodzianko, president of the Duma, advocated working out a compromise with the socialists. Milyukov was a politician who favored consolidating relations with the Allies and opposed the supremacy of the Soviets.

CHAPTER 15 **THE REVOLUTION**

1. Charles de Chambrun, *Lettres à Marie, Pétersbourg-Petrograd, 1914–1918.*

2. Victor Serge, *Memoirs of a Revolutionary.* (London: Oxford University Press, 1963).

3. Maria Andreyeva held many official positions in the Soviet Union and died in 1953, at the age of eighty-one. Ekaterina Peshkov also had a distinguished career in her country. She died, held in high esteem, in 1965, at eighty-seven.

4. Deniken and Kolchak were prominent czarist generals; Rodzyanko was a politician, head of the Octobrist Party.

CHAPTER 17 **THE OFFICIAL SPOKESMAN**

1. Victor Serge, *Memoirs of a Revolutionary.* (London: Oxford University Press, 1963).

INDEX